THE ART OF BOAT NAMES
Inspiring ideas for names and designs

An ironic solution or a missed opportunity?

THE ART OF BOAT NAMES
Inspiring ideas for names and designs

LAURIE CHURCHMAN

International Marine/McGraw-Hill
Camden, Maine ▪ New York ▪ Chicago ▪ San Francisco ▪
Lisbon ▪ London ▪ Madrid ▪ Mexico City ▪ Milan ▪ New
Delhi ▪ San Juan ▪ Seoul ▪ Singapore ▪ Sydney ▪ Toronto

The McGraw-Hill Companies

1 2 3 4 5 6 7 8 9 RRD SHEN 0 9

Library of Congress Cataloging-in-Publication Data may
be found at the Library of Congress.

ISBN 978-0-07-159142-3
MHID 0-07-159142-7

Questions regarding the content of this book
should be addressed to
International Marine
www.internationalmarine.com

Questions regarding the ordering of this book
should be addressed to
The McGraw-Hill Companies
Customer Service Department
P.O. Box 547
Blacklick, OH 43004
Retail customers: 1-800-262-4729
Bookstores: 1-800-722-4726

International Marine/McGraw-Hill books are available at
special quantity discounts to use as premiums or for use
in training programs. For more information please visit
the Contact Us pages at internationalmarine.com

Credits and permissions may be found on page 170,
which constitutes an extension of this copyright page.

Book editing: Jonathan Eaton
Book design: Laurie Churchman
Primary typefaces: Scala family designed by Martin Majoor
and Univers Family designed by Adrian Frutiger.

for my parents

contents

Tenacity

acknowledgments

My first thanks go to Nancy Green who believed it was possible to talk about boating and typography under the same book cover, and was gracious enough to pass my idea onto editor Jon Eaton at International Marine. And to Jon for taking it on, and with Molly Mulhern, wisely and with good humor, shaping it. Their expertise has been invaluable.

Nautical history and even contemporary boating are far outside my area of knowledge; therefore I have gleaned much from the expertise of Lionel Casson, Ian Friel, Fred Hocker, Dilwyn Jones, and William Murray, along with the collections at Mariners' Museum, Mystic Seaport Museum, and Independence Seaport Museum. A special thanks to Megan Fraser and Matt Herbison at Independence Seaport Museum for granting me the many weeks necessary to search their collection. And to Luc Bernard whose chance meeting encouraged the first step in my research.

My humblest thanks to the many contributors without whom this book wouldn't have progressed beyond a good idea. To all of the letterers who gave so generously of their time and openly of their work: Renee Anderson, Carla Christopher, Bud Gillespie, Joe Hessmann, Cindy Fletcher-Holden, Lisa Hutchinson, Howard Rogers, Ray Skaines, and Bobby Thomas (posthumously). To Dan Husted whose beautiful photographs enliven so many pages, and who went the distance in ideas, travel, and support. To Jim Garballey, Joseph Butera Sr., and the students at Butera School of Art, who gave me a new appreciation for the craft of lettering by letting me watch them work. To Scott Hunt for his thoughtful feedback and support throughout the process. To all of the dedicated typographers whose typefaces we admire throughout this book. And to the countless other letterers, artists, designers, and boatowners whose names I documented but wasn't able to properly attribute.

The book would have been impossible without the support of my colleagues at the University of Pennsylvania and, the extraordinary efforts of my student researchers Emmy Hoy and Kat Coneybear.

My parents, family, and friends come last, not as an afterthought, instead with the utmost gratitude. Your ongoing encouragement, anticipation, and interest has meant everything.

preface

I should start by confessing that I'm what is referred to in graphic design parlance as a "type nerd"—meaning that I'm keenly interested in lettering and typography, to put a pleasant spin on it. When I look at a boat transom, my first questions are not why it's shaped as it is or what sort of engine might be lurking on the other side of it, but rather how the boat's name was chosen and why the name is set in that particular typestyle. *We all have our obsessions.*

My interest in boat names originated, as any true inspiration can, from a lovely day on the water. I noticed that the names and graphics on the boats I was encountering ran the gamut from dull to truly inspired. This brush with letterform varieties on the sea got my attention and raised a few questions. Those questions led first to a hilarious conversation with a boat broker at a bar in the Abacos, and then to a few years of research that taught me far more about nautical life than I could have imagined. After time I realized that, although there have been two or three books listing suggested names for boats, nothing had been written about the visual design of boat names.

As a designer, I see a boat's name and lettering as a first impression at the very least, and ideally as a unique opportunity for personal expression. I maintain that the choice and design of your boat's name communicates as much about you as the style of your boat does. There are so many options today that it should be interesting, if not compelling, to think about who you are and what you want to say through your boat's name and its design.

So this is an idea book. In Chapter One I've compiled a brief history of naming traditions from ancient Egypt to the present, in part because I found it fascinating and otherwise unavailable from any single source, but also in part because it provides a context for what follows. We tend to think of names as floating up from our contemporary cultural soup, when in fact the names we use today partake of a rich maritime history.

The remaining three chapters explore the design and application of boat lettering and graphics. I've included a host of images and names to make this book a visual resource too. The discussion of design styles (Chapter Two) and design principles (Chapter Three) invite you to develop your boat's unique personality visually. And Chapter Four is here to guide you through the more practical application choices from hand painting to illuminated dimensional lettering.

While researching this book I interviewed many professional boat letterers, and I've included as interludes between chapters a few of their stories. Many talented artists and designers create boat graphics, but their work is rarely identified. Their backstories—like those of other service providers—are fascinating and sometimes enlightening. The stories selected here are shared through the generosity of the letterers themselves, who invited me into their studios and explained the nuances of their work.

Also bookending the chapters are ten galleries of boat names and images. These are just a small sampling of what can be seen on the water and at the dock in any harbor. The tens of millions of boats in the United States alone provide an overwhelming number of potential examples. Not every name illustrated here is stellar; what I've tried to assemble is a diverse, representative, entertaining, instructive sampling, not a best of show. The majority of the images are from the East Coast of the United States because that is where my travels have taken me. Another book could be compiled simply comparing boat-naming tendencies on the East Coast, the Great Lakes, the West Coast, the Caribbean, the Mediterranean, England, northern Europe, and elsewhere in the world. I'm certain there are regional nuances to be enjoyed.

Permit me a note about terms. Boat lettering formerly referenced the act of hand painting letters on a transom or topsides, but now it is as likely or more likely to refer to the application of vinyl or off-the-shelf dimensional letters. Boat graphics and marine graphics are newer terms used by website companies and sign shops, sometimes with reference to images only. Boat lettering and graphics is sometimes the preferred phrasing when a commercial service wants to unambiguously offer both, but really the two terms—lettering and graphics—are interchangeable these days. Either one is understood to include both letters and images, and that is the sense in which I use "boat lettering" in this book.

Similarly, in most instances I identify the creator of a design as a letterer, even though he or she may consider himself an artist, designer, letterer, sign painter, or none of the above. I like "letterer" as a descriptor because it's compatible with boat lettering.

The world of boats was something of a mystery to me five years ago. Through this book I've come to appreciate the beauty, tranquility, excitement, pleasure, history, spirit, and toil of boat ownership. Above all, I've come to appreciate the elusive magic of boats.

Swash Capital Letters

Ligatures (the deliberate joining of letters)

Dropshadow

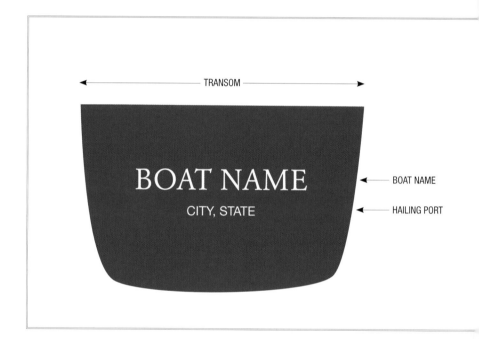

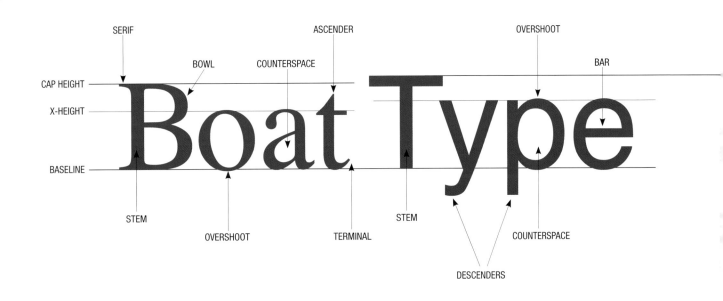

SERIF   ASCENDER   OVERSHOOT

BOWL   COUNTERSPACE   BAR

CAP HEIGHT

X-HEIGHT

BASELINE

STEM   OVERSHOOT   TERMINAL   STEM   COUNTERSPACE

DESCENDERS

Boat is set in the serif typeface Times at 120 point.

Type is set in the sans serif typeface Helvetica Regular at 120 point.

she's called...

A SWEETIE · AFTER YOU · ALMOST A LADY · ALEXIS · ALL HERS · ALTHEA · AMAZING GRACE · AMIGA · ANGEL · ANGIE BABY · ANOTHER GIRL · APHRODITE · AQUA LADY · ARABELLA · ARIEL · ASIAN QUEEN · AWESOME LADY · BABY · BABY CAKES · BABY DOLL · BAHAMA MAMA · BARB WIRE · BELLA · BELLE · BESSIE · BIG MAMA · BLONDIE · BLUE BELLE · BLUE EYES · BLUE JEAN · BO PEEP · BOSS LADY · BROWN-EYED-GIRL · CALAMITY JANE · CAREER GIRL · CARIBBEAN LADY · CARIBBEAN QUEEN · CAUSE FOR DIVORCE · CHAQUITA · CHERIE · CHICKADEE · CHICKSDIGIT · CHINA DOLL · CLAIREBUOYANT · CLASSY LADY · COMPASS ROSE · CONSTANCE · CONTESSA · CORRINA · COSMIC LADY · COUNTESS · COVER GIRL · COWGIRL · CRAZY LADY · CRYSTAL · CURRENT WIFE · DAISY · DAMSEL · DANCER · DARK LADY · DEAR JANE · DELTA DAWN · DIVA · DOLL · DOLL BABY · DRAGON LADY · DREAMBOAT · DREAM GIRL · DUTCHESS · EPOXY QUEEN · FISH-N-CHICKS · FISHWIFE · FLUSIE · FOXY LADY · GIRLS' TOY · GOLDEN GIRL · GRAPHIC LADY · GULF LADY · HER MISTRESS · HER RING · HI HONEY · HONEY'S MONEY · IT'S A GIRL! · JEZEBELLE · JOY-SEA · LADY M LEAKIN' · LENA · LUSCIOUS LADY · MA'AM · MADAME X · MA HONEY · MAIDEN · MAIN SQUEEZE · MAJESTIC BEAUTY · MAMA MIA · MARLIN MONROE · MATCHMAKER ·

Krishelle

Mrs. Tracy

Carrie B

Amy A

Jackie O

CAROL ANN

SADIE

Miss Donna

JANET

By far, female names are still the traditionally styled. Transoms featuring scripts or serif typestyles prevail, and the classic colors of gold and black are amply applied. In more contemporary scripts, capital letters are replaced by upper- and lowercase letters with the intent of maintaining a feminine and simple design.

Janie, lettered in a bold sans serif, stands out for its modern design although the gold color and crown graphic soften its overall appearance. *Jackie O* takes a whimsical approach more commonly seen on sportfishing boats. And *Alice* represents the creativity of old-school hand painting.

MAY QUEEN · MELIKA · MERMAID · MILADY · MISS ADVENTURE · MISS APPROPRIATION · MISS BEHAVIN · MISS CONDUCT ·

MISS FITS · MISS FORTUNE · MISS GOODY TWO SCREWS · MISS GUIDED · MISS MY MONEY · MISS PRIORITY · MISS SASSIFIED ·

MISS TRIAL · MISTRESS · MOMMA'S MINK · MY GIRL · MY OLD LADY · MYSTERY LADY · NANSEA · NERVOUS NELLIE · NIMBLE

LASS · NOTORIOUS LADY · NYMPH · OH BABY · OLD LADY · OLD MAID · PANDORA · PAPER DOLL · PARTY GIRL · PATIENT LADY ·

PINK LADY · PLAY GIRL · POLYANNA · PRETTY GIRL · PRETTY PENNY · PRINCESS OF THE SEA · PROUD MARY · PUSSYCAT ·

QUEEN ANN'S REVENGE · QUEEN BEE · QUEEN OF HEARTS · RAPTURESS · RAPUNZEL · REBELLIOUS LADY · RED HOT MAMA · REEL

LADY · RIVER LADY · ROBIN'S NEST · ROSEBUD · SALTY GAL · SAUCY · SCARLET · SEA NO RITA · SEA QUEEN · SEA WENCH · SEA WIFE ·

SEA WITCH · SECOND HAND ROSE · SENORITA · SHADY LADY · SHE BANG · SHE DEVIL · SHE GOT THE HOUSE · SHE'LL GET OVER IT ·

SHE MIGHT · SHE WOLF · SHE-WORTHY · SHIRLEY'S TEMPLE · SILVER QUEEN · SISTER · SISTERWIND · SLEEPING BEAUTY · SLO

BABE · SOO DOO VOODOO · SOUTHERN BELLE · SUE SEA · SUGAR MAMA · SUN MAID · SUNSHINE GIRL · SUSIE QUEUE · SWEET LI'L

SIXTEEN · TARA · TATTOOED LADY · TEMPTRESS · THAT'S ALL SHE WROTE · THE OTHER WOMAN · TIGER LILY · TOOTSIE · TRAMP ·

ULTIMATE WOMAN · VINTAGE LADY · VIXEN · WIDOW'S KISS · WILD HONEY · WONDER GIRL · YANKEE GIRL · YES DEAR

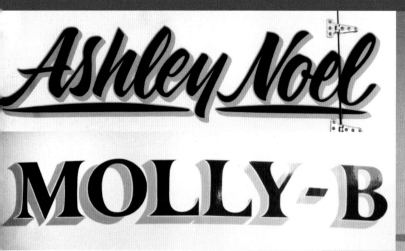

Contrary Mary is hand-painted in the traditional Cuban style of southern Florida. Its swash letters and filigree nicely integrate all elements of the name. Using swash capital letters, as seen in several names below, can add visual interest and weight to the design.

Norma Jean uses atypical blackletter typography. With roots in the Middle Ages, this typestyle has formal qualities that may be too much for some names or boat types.

Miss Jimi

Peggy Sue Two

MARY

THON, FLA.

Dardanella

LONDON

TRINA

MADISONVILLE, LA

Norma Jean

Janet Ann

Emily's Freedom

A painting of Odysseus's ship on an Athenian vase from the late sixth or early fifth century BC shows Odysseus lashed to the mast while he and his men pass the Sirens. The *udjat eye* painted on the bow was a common decoration used to protect a vessel and safeguard a voyage.

The naming of possessions has a long history, from which the names of ancient warships may be among the earliest examples. Today we are surrounded by objects that have been named by their owners as a way to ascribe personality, advertise ownership, or simply ease identification. Boats, cars, houses, and even computer hard drives are named. But though a car might be *Old Bessie,* a beach house *Sun Spot,* or a hard drive *Big Mac,* you are unlikely to see the name visually displayed on the object, and even when the name appears, it is unlikely to have a deliberate design style. Boat names are the exception. Their visual representation is often an integral part of the identity of the boat and its owner, and this is truer today than ever. Contemporary pleasure-boat names range from family namesakes to funny nicknames and from concrete to conceptual. One might be the fourth version of the same name, another an ephemeral ID utilized between owners.

In contrast, ancient ship names were of a different order. The emphasis wasn't outwardly personal or self-referential on the part of the ship's owner, and there was no place for names such as *Wet Spot, Bite Me, or Vitamin Sea.* Rather, names were primarily functional, or they combined function with a descriptor that glorified a deity.

To give better context to our current naming conventions, it is instructive to survey some of the traditions of naming and seafaring.

chapter one
A BRIEF HISTORY OF NAMING

A model boat found in Tutankhamen's tomb shows the high level of decoration on Egyptian ships—especially painted patterning—but no visible name.

AN ANCIENT TRADITION

The earliest history of ship names is not well documented, and where names can be found they are usually included in ancient naval or commercial records. Still, ship names have been documented from as early as 1500 BC. Although *Argo*, the ship from Greek mythology that carried Jason and the Argonauts, is often referenced as the earliest named ship, Egyptians were naming warships well before that voyage. Ancient Egyptian naval inventories show ship names that honored their god-kings in a variety of ways. Pharaohs' names were used singly or in conjunction with adulatory descriptors. *Ramses II Who Propitiates the Aton* (Aton being a deity) and *Amenhotep II Who Made Strong the Two Lands* were among the names in the navy lists. Less commonly, ships were named after animals—as in *The Fishes*—or as a tribute to the pharaoh's success—as in *Star in Both Lands.* None of these names has been found on a preserved vessel; they are known only through records—although decorative patterns and symbols such as the lotus flower and *udjat* eyes were common in Egypt's New Kingdom (1550–1070 BC) and are seen on model boats, in paintings, and on reliefs. This decoration held meaning, often as a means to ensure a safe voyage, but did not represent the name of the boat. Model boats found in Tutankhamen's tomb feature some of the best-documented examples of these early design motifs and symbols.

Lionel Casson's book *Ships and Seamanship in the Ancient World* is a wealth of information on naming conventions from Egyptian to Roman times. In it he outlines interesting distinctions between Egyptian and early Greek practices of warship naming. While Egyptian warships were nearly always named for their god-kings, Greeks before the fourth century BC favored lesser mythological figures and shunned direct reference to major deities. Single-word attributes of a ship were popular among the Greeks, such as *Charis* for "grace," *Aglaia* for "beauty," or *Chrsye* for "golden." Names of minor heroines or sea nymphs, such as Nereus, were also favored, as were abstract ideals such as *Dynamis* for "power." *Nike* for "victory" was a particular favorite. And as is done today, the most popular names were used on multiple ships. Other Greek names were taken from geography, animals, politics, and city life, though these were less common. Names specific to an individual or a shipowner were not used.

All names in early Greece were written in the feminine form, so the characteristic use of "she" when referring to a vessel has a long history. This doesn't mean that all names were female, only that the feminine form of the chosen word was used. The origin of this practice is uncertain, but it may have been an attempt to appease or please the gods. Since Poseidon was the male god of the seas, known not only for his power but for his philandering, mariners may have believed that presenting their vessels as feminine could make them more attractive to the god, thereby ensuring a safer voyage.

From the Hellenistic rulers (323 BC) through the time of Roman ascendance, navy ships were named after powerful dignitaries, deities, and figures from mythology. Roman ship names included *Hercules, Apollo,* and *Nereis* along with such descriptive names as *Radians* (gleaming) and *Triumphus* "success." Strong or war-like animals such as *Taurus* (bull) and *Draco* (dragon) provided additional sources of inspiration. Although Romans took their ship-naming cues from the Greeks, they used male forms of names as frequently as female forms. Strictly feminine names were no longer the accepted practice.

Though names of ancient naval ships can sometimes be ascertained from surviving documents, coins, gravemarkers, artwork, and nautical archaeologists' finds, it is harder to determine whether those names appeared on the ships themselves. Ancient vessels were adorned with intricate carvings, markings, and paintings on the prow and stern, some of which were used as identifying devices and were called *parasemon,* or, literally, "name devices." Historians believe that these carvings and markings served in lieu of lettered names as visual identifiers. A name device positioned on either side of the bow was more likely to represent the ship's given name than devices found elsewhere on the vessel, which might instead represent a guardian deity for the ship. Name devices, because of their large size, would have been easier to see than written names and did not require the viewer to be literate.

In this stone relief of a two-banked Roman galley from the second half of the first century BC, the carved head encompassed in a boxed frame represents, and honors, a deity.

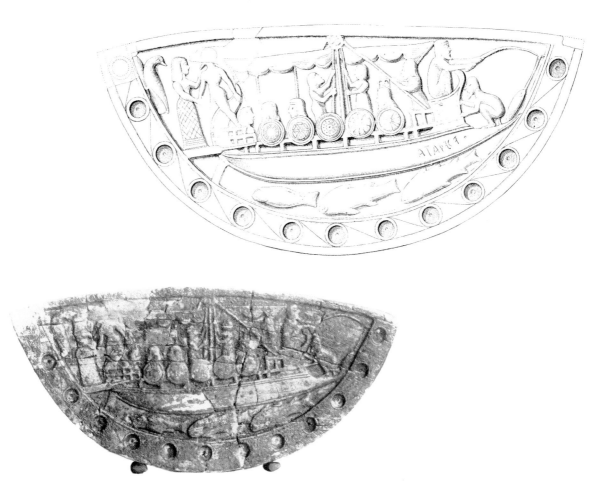

At top is a drawing based on an ivory plaque found at the Temple of Artemis Orthia in Sparta, Greece, 650–600 BC. In a relief of this plaque, the word "Orthaia" is inscribed on the bow reading left to right (shown here in reverse). It can only be speculated that *Orthaia* was the name of the ship as well as the goddess. Below is a photograph of the original ivory plaque, with only "AIA" barely visible.

Still, some historians and nautical archaeologists believe that lettered names were inscribed on ships as early as 480 BC. Historian William Murray has documented use of the Greek term *ptychë* in the third century BC to denote the place on the prow of a ship where its name was inscribed. An ancient wall drawing from that era shows the name *Isis* inscribed in the *ptychë* of a warship, and the precise rendering of the engraved letters with their flared terminals suggests that the name was an important part of the ship's detailing.

In Athens, the Themistocles Decree of 480 BC called for ship names to be posted publicly above the names of their assigned crews. Without ship names to direct Athenian citizens to their vessels, Murray noted, there would have been "chaos as 40,000 men tried to find their way to 200 Athenian vessels designated *solely* by figural plaques." The implication is that ship names were displayed on the ships themselves, because it is hard to imagine that name devices alone could suffice— especially in a large fleet of vessels at port or at sea, and particularly given that ships sometimes shared the same name or possessed abstract, difficult-to-symbolize names.

Nearly all the recorded names from ancient times are from warships, though the few known references to merchant or private boat names suggest that these followed the same naming conventions. Surviving drawings of such vessels lack enough detail to show a name on the hull, if one existed.

Based on the writing conventions of Greek and Roman times, we can suppose that when a name was inscribed on a ship it appeared in all capital letters finished with the wedge serifs typical of chiseled letterforms. Straight lines were easier to chisel than curves, an early example of how writing tools influence the appearance of letters, even though the ship name would most likely have been painted, not carved, on the hull. Wedge-style serifs provided needed finishing strokes to improve legibility. Such letterforms, referred to as square capitals today, were the formal writing style of the era and are typified by the writing chiseled into famous Roman antiquities such as Trajan's Column. Modern typefaces such as Lithos and Trajan model the Greek and Roman letterform styles.

When a name was inscribed on a hull or on a nameboard attached to a hull, the likely position for it would have been the above-mentioned *ptychë* on either side of the bow. The transom stern so familiar today didn't exist in ancient ships, which were double-ended, so it is unlikely that names were displayed aft. Also, in depictions of ancient ships, nearly all are represented in side view, so it is difficult to know whether or not any names were positioned directly on the stem or stern finials.

LITHOS—ΙΣΙΣ

ISIS set in Lithos. This font, designed by Carol Twombly in 1989, was inspired by Greek inscriptional letters.

TRAJAN

Trajan, also designed by Carol Twombly in 1989, was inspired by the chiseled letters of Trajan's Column in Rome.

Chiseled letters on a Greek column from the Post-Herulian wall, third century BC.

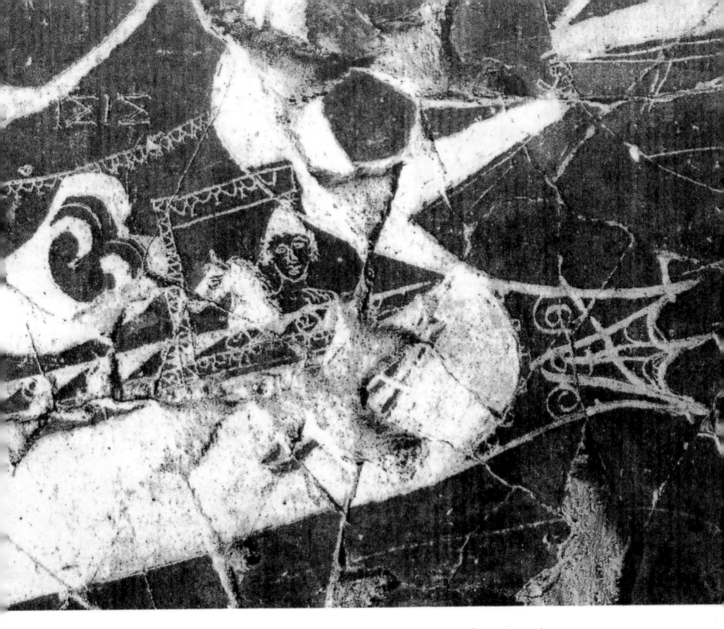

This drawing found in Nymphaion, Greece, dates to the third century BC and shows the inscription of the name *Isis* in a position consistent with a *ptychë*.

STAYING THE COURSE

After the fall of the Roman Empire, navies and merchant shipping became far more decentralized. Someone could write an interesting history comparing the ship-naming traditions that developed in the Middle Ages in Europe, Scandinavia, the Middle East, and the Far East—though English traditions would ultimately have the most direct effect on ship naming in America.

As with many other records in the Middle Ages, ship documents in England were not well kept by individual territories or rulers. Even visual sources are scarce, with European illuminated manuscripts among the few. Ships were sometimes included as part of a narrative or an allegory in manuscripts, but these can't be relied upon for accurate depictions. Names do not appear on renderings of ships, though the illustrations were highly colored and complex. It's not known if names were simply left out or didn't appear on the ships, but the latter seems more likely because the illustrations were detailed in other respects. Like ancient illustrations of ships, these show a double-ended hull construction, meaning that any name on a hull should have been visible in a side-view depiction. (Ships were depicted in side view in part because perspective wasn't well utilized as a drawing method until later. In addition, a side view offered the greatest detail as seen from shore, and combat took place with ships lying side by side, so this was also the most familiar and critical view for representation.)

While English history wove its way through land battles, conquerors, a succession of ruling parties, and the advancement of Christianity during the Middle Ages, seafaring remained active. Warships attempted to fend off invaders such as the Vikings, while merchant ships traded goods across Europe. Still, there were few advances in ship design and construction in the Middle Ages, and the notion of pleasure boating was still unknown. Any small, personal watercraft that did exist were utilitarian and without visible names. Ian Friel's book *The Good Ship* offers a detailed history of ships and seafaring during this era.

Most naval and merchant ships in medieval times were given religious or proper names. Saints' names were popular, and when common names were used they might be female or (less frequently) male. Both feminine and masculine articles were used with names, often irrespective of the gender of the name. *Mary* and *Virgin Mary* were ubiquitous, and there were many *Margaret*s and *Katherine*s.

Above A roundel decorating the opening chapter of Genesis in a French bible, 1220–40 AD. Depicting Noah's ark, it shows a double-ended hull.

Right Another illustration of Noah's ark from an illuminated scroll detailing the genealogy of Edward IV, 1461 AD.

17

LE
TON'ANT

Though used less often, male names included *Philippe, George, Thomas,* and *Peter.* Merchant ships favored proper names, though the variation among those names was rather small.

Religious references became even more prevalent in the late Middle Ages and into the 1400s, particularly for the royal ships of Kings Henry IV and Henry V. *Jesus Maria, Holigost, Jesus, Grace Dieu,* and *Trinity Royal* are representative of the names of their ships. Names also included descriptors of the type of ship, whether cog, bark, carvel, or simply ship, as in *St. Mary Cog* or *Great Bark.* Compound names such as *Malice-Scourge, War-Spite,* and *Mary Rose* became especially popular for warships and merchant ships during the Elizabethan era.

From the mid-1400s into the 1500s, an evolution in the construction of large ships introduced flat sterns, in part to house gunports. The new sterns became quite ornate and often included transom windows, galleries, and elaborately carved emblems and royal crests. These carvings made ideal identifiers, especially for the origin of the ship, but were not used for the depiction of the ship's name. Other intricate carvings told stories of battles, geography, history, and ownership—some with great drama and craftsmanship. Names, if included at all, were lettered on plaques or cartouche panels positioned within the carved designs. Other ship identifiers included flags, or pennants, flying from the masts. These were most often the flag or emblem of the ship's country of origin.

It is curious, given the beauty and detail embodied in stern designs, that the name of the ship wasn't considered an integral element in the design. That it wasn't suggests that a ship's name was, first and foremost, for utilitarian identification, not for some more expressive purpose. Explanations for chosen names are rare in the records; they are simply stated without elaboration. One of the most ornate ships ever built in England was the *Sovereign of the Seas.* Built in 1637, the most powerful warship of her time, she was adorned with breathtaking allegorical carvings and other decorative elements and gilding—but no visible name on the stern.

Ship portraiture began in the late fifteenth century and expanded throughout the Renaissance. Such portraits were commissioned by a ship's merchant-owner or by the ruler of a navy. Earnest depictions meant to feature a ship to best advantage, they could be showy or simply documentary and were displayed for personal status or used to help sell a merchant ship. Such portraits, along with Dutch engravings of the seventeenth and eighteenth centuries, have left a rich visual

Le Tonant's name is featured in a carved plaque applied to a highly decorated stern. It is more of an add-on than an integral part of the transom design.

verscheide soorten

HOLLANDSE VAARTUIGEN

6de Catern

door G: Groenewegen 1791

F   een Poon met een Paveljoen.

record of ships of that period. Several Dutch marine artists created series in which a different ship was drawn in detail on each individual plate. These drawings are considered accurate; one of the artists, Gerrit Groenewegen, was particularly well known for the accuracy of his renderings, some of which included names. His drawings "A Greenlander running free" and "A Poon with a Stateroom" from the late 1700s show names clearly.

In Groenewegen's drawings, names were rendered in all capital letters and appear to be in serif-style letterforms, in keeping with the ancient tradition and with the writing styles then still in use throughout Europe. Capital letters (majuscules) were the accepted standard for formal writing in the seventeenth and eighteenth centuries, though lowercase serifed letters, referred to as minuscules, had developed during the late Roman Empire. Minuscules were an outgrowth of quicker, more informal handwriting and were adopted and adapted by various countries. Use of minuscules waxed and waned through the Middle Ages before coming into more common usage during the Renaissance. That ships' names remained in all capital letters signifies their categorization as proper names. During the Renaissance, names or titles appeared in capital letters in written communications.

Drawings and engravings don't offer many clues about boat lettering on personal watercraft or pleasure boats. Small personal watercraft or fishing boats are depicted, especially in harbor scenes, but they are never shown with any ornament or identifying markings. Pleasure boats remained a rarity until well into the 1700s in Europe and the 1800s in the United States. An anonymous Dutch engraving *Een Speel-jacht* dated 1640 gives a rare glimpse of the earliest yachting.

"A Poon with a Stateroom" by Gerrit Groenewegen, 1791. This passenger ship has a name on the stern, probably on a carved nameboard, in serifed capital letters.

The inscription reads: "Earnings which are often increased by sailing in trade, Are consumed again in sailing for pleasure." The yacht flies the Dutch flag in three places yet doesn't appear to have a lettered name or nameboard on its bow or transom stern.

Records of ships with visible names are easier to find beginning in the 1700s. Marine artists in England, many of whom emigrated to the United States, painted ship portraits and marine scenes to earn money. Not all can be taken as accurate depictions, because the pride of the vessel's owner often influenced how dramatically or realistically a painting was rendered. Still, there are enough paintings and drawings after this time to show that the practice of painting names either directly onto sterns or onto decorative plaques that were then mounted on sterns was becoming general. The reigning style remained all capital letters in a serif typeface. In some cases the baseline of the text was arched to follow the lines of the stern. On plaques or cartouches the name might be stacked in two lines, depending on the size and length of the name.

Passengers appear to be enjoying a relaxed sail in *Een Speel-jacht,* 1640. There is no visible boat name on the transom stern or strakes.

Een Speel-jacht

T'geen dickwils 't varen heeft vermeert
Wert dus al varende verteert

ON TO AMERICA

Prior to 1698, English ships doing business with America were required to be registered with a name and to initiate a new registration for a name change, indicating that named boats were a familiar part of the American seascape. England's Navigation Act of 1699 required registration of British-built ships but didn't specify any display of the name or port of the ship. An act of Parliament in 1786 made it obligatory to paint the name on the stern of a British-built merchant ship, in letters four inches tall, within the first month after registration. The act made no mention of requiring a home port. In the United States, one of the early acts passed by the First Congress in 1789 required the registering and clearing of all American commercial vessels. The act included no requirement for displaying the name on a vessel, but the name and home port appeared in the vessel document.

The utilitarian lettering of *Edith* and *Defiance,* contrasted with the commercial appeal of *Escort*'s lettering, exemplifies the range of design styles available by the late 1880s and early 1900s. *Edith* and *Defiance,* 1911, are roughly painted—dark letters on a light hull—for simple identification, while the name *Escort,* from this painting by James Edward Butterworth from the mid-1880s, is amply and inconsistently applied on a nameboard next to the pilothouse (yellow letters, probably sans serif), as an "E" on the bow flag (white sans serif), and decoratively in front of the paddle wheel (red serif letters with a thick yellow dropshadow and a period for emphasis).

Until the 1800s almost all U.S. nonmilitary boats were merchant (commercial) boats used to fish, haul cargo, or provide transportation. There were few recreational vessels, although working boats were sometimes pressed into service as pleasure boats for short trips. Commercial or "working" boats generally had simple names rendered in simple lettering styles. The purpose of the name was to provide identification, not ornament; therefore the name was hand-painted in all capital letters in plain serif or sans serif type on either side of the bow.

Passenger steamboats came to constitute a unique exception to the rule of straightforward lettering. Many paddle steamers sported large and decorative typography on the paddle wheel cover or on a solid piece of walling between the deck railings. Letters were painted in bright colors with dramatic dropshadows and outlines. The lettering reflected nineteenth-century advertising type and utilized slab serifs, extended and condensed letterforms, and decorative typefaces, the better to appeal to travelers.

Above *Nourmahal II* (motoryacht) was built in 1921 for Vincent Astor. The name and hailing port are painted in sans serif bold capitals with an arched baseline that emphasizes the curve of the counter stern. The name is also repeated on a nameboard on the pilot house.

Right *Flirt,* in a detail and photograph taken in Philadelphia, 1875. Breaking from tradition, the design is similar to a modern logo in the way it integrates text and artwork.

BOATING FOR PLEASURE

Not until the mid-1800s was there a demand for small boats—mostly sailboats or personal watercraft such as rowboats and canoes—for leisure-time use on lakes and waterways. An act of Congress in 1848 acknowledged the increasing number of pleasure vessels by requiring them to be licensed and to use signal flags. After 1866 documented vessels were required to have an official number.

Following the advent of the gas engine in the late 1880s, the popularity of pleasure boating increased so dramatically that by the turn of the century it had become a true consumer industry. Few small boats displayed names, however, due to their limited size for lettering as well as a lack of regulations requiring names for small watercraft. Small boats were considered more accessories than significant personal possessions.

At the same time, however, large motor and sailing yachts were being built for recreational use and exploratory adventures. These yachts could be afforded only by the wealthy merchant class and were built with status in mind—and they were also very much a man's domain. Cornelius Vanderbilt is credited with the first American motor yacht, which he named *North Star*. The "Sayings and Doings" column of *Harper's Bazaar* in 1870 noted that the "disposition to engage in yachting as an amusement has greatly increased within a few years, although the expenses of maintaining an ordinary yacht are not inconsiderable." The author goes on to cite four yachts—*Dauntless, Cambria,*

Fleetwing, and *Calypso*—the most expensive of which, *Dauntless,* was said to cost $65,000. Mentions of personal and social yachting activities became common entries in *Harper's Bazaar* society–related columns. When in 1928 *Time* magazine did a full-length article on William Vincent Astor's new yacht, even featuring him on the cover, there is mention of the possible name, *Nourmahal* after several previous Astor family yachts. The cost was estimated at up to two million dollars, with annual upkeep of over $100,000.

Steamships of the late 1800s and early 1900s had typical names, many of them female *(Isabel, Jeannette)* and many of them from history or mythology *(Electra, Delphine, Aphrodite).* Larger sloops of the period had names such as *Mist, Maria, Alpha, Undine, May Flower, Bianca, Irene, Ripple, Mary,* and *Gertrude.* There were a few unconventional names too, including *Say When,* built in 1888, and *Flirt,* seen in an 1875 photograph. *Flirt's* creative lettering is unusual for the time, though tame by current standards. Pictured on the bow, the name may or may not have been repeated on the stern.

Yacht names were well documented starting in the late nineteenth century. In the spirit of *Lloyd's Register of Ships* in Britain, a published listing of American pleasure yachts, *The American Yacht List,* began in 1881. Taken over by *Lloyd's* in 1903, it was renamed *Lloyd's Register of American Yachts.* While the register by no means contained all names, and the inclusion of names had differing criteria over time, it made trend-spotting possible. Female names were still very common in 1906, with *Alice* and *Margaret* as favorites. *As You Like It, Skeidaddle,*

AMERICA'S CUP NAMES

America	1851	USA
Magic	1870	USA
Columbia/Sappho	1871	USA
Madeleine	1876	USA
Mischief	1881	USA
Puritan	1885	USA
Mayflower	1886	USA
Volunteer	1887	USA
Vigilant	1893	USA
Defender	1895	USA
Columbia	1899	USA
Columbia	1901	USA
Reliance	1903	USA
Resolute	1920	USA
Enterprise	1930	USA
Rainbow	1934	USA
Ranger	1937	USA
Columbia	1958	USA
Weatherly	1962	USA
Constellation	1964	USA
Intrepid	1967	USA
Intrepid	1970	USA
Courageous	1974	USA
Courageous	1977	USA
Freedom	1980	USA
Australia II	1983	Australia
Stars & Stripes	1987	USA
Stars & Stripes	1988	USA
America3	1992	USA
Black Magic	1995	New Zealand
Black Magic	2000	New Zealand
Alinghi	2003	Switzerland
Alinghi	2007	Switzerland

Beat It, and *Truant* represented some of the most nontraditional on the list. There were five yachts named *Truant.*

Racing yachts might be expected to have had more adventurous names, reflecting the challenges of competition, but judging from early America's Cup winners, this didn't hold true. *America,* the 1851 winner that established the contest, was followed in the 1880s by *Mischief, Puritan, Mayflower,* and *Volunteer* and at the turn of the century by *Columbia,* a two-time winner. These were followed by other resonant but fairly ordinary names, such as *Reliance, Resolute, Enterprise, Rainbow,* and *Ranger,* before another *Columbia* returned in 1958. Though they represented a break from female names or those pulled from mythology, these names weren't innovative or daring, and their lettering was equally staid. The standard design used hand-lettered capital letters in a modern serif typeface such as Bodoni.

SAME NAME GAME

Given the long history of naming, it's no surprise that even in 1874 yacht owners tried hard to find appropriate names for their newly built yachts. According to one *Harper's Bazaar* story, an owner "asked a literary friend for a good name to give [his yacht]. 'Something un-hackneyed, you know, and yet descriptive.' The reply met the case. 'Call it O, si sic Omnes!' That is, in English, 'Would you were all like this!' or, which will perhaps be quite as appropriate, we may translate it, 'Oh, seasick Omnes!' " A 1910 article in the popular magazine *MotorBoating* lamented a lack of creativity in naming, citing the overuse of female, seabird, and fish names. "A good boat is worthy of a name that will distinguish it from others," the writer argued, but "many popular appellations are worn threadbare and lack individuality."

By 1920 a small motorboat was no more expensive than a car, and the resultant greater demand led to more repetition in naming. That demand also spurred the U.S. Numbering Act of 1918, under which all undocumented vessels measuring over 16 feet and propelled in whole or in part by machinery were to secure a certificate of a number. A name on the stern was recommended but not required, but the number had to be displayed on the bow in block letters no less than three inches tall. Exceptions to the rule included public vessels, boats measuring 16 feet or under, and boats that were only temporarily equipped with outboard motors.

Built in 1929 for Winthrop
W. Aldrich, *Wayfarer* has
sans serif lettering more
typical of a simple work-
ing boat. The letterer of
this name could have used
a lesson in proper letterspacing—note how close
together the letters "W,"
"A," and "Y" are in
comparison with "FARER."
The wider spacing is pre-
ferred for legibility.

"WE SCUDDED ON TOWARD CHESAPEAK

This page from the Kleinschmidt family's 1907 cruise scrapbook humorously reminisces about their time aboard *White Seal* and *Helen*. Both boats' names are surrounded by interesting carved scrollwork. *White Seal*'s three-dimensional capital letters are in a decorative typestyle with curves that match the scrollwork.

Nameboards were as common as painted letters for the display of names. Like the simple name treatments on ornately carved sterns of Renaissance ships, nameboards were simple too. Often a carved or filigreed border enclosed plain carved letters. Two examples of this style from 1907 are *White Seal* and *Helen,* shown here docked in Maryland.

Conventional names still dominated the 1925 *Lloyd's Register of American Yachts.* Anything using the word "sea" *(See Bee, Sea Dog, Seafarer, Sea Puss, Seaward)* was popular. Among the unconventional names were *Hoodathunkit, Kumalong, Miss Donuts,* and *You'll Do.* For the most part, however, these names were recorded only in text. Though photography was mainstream by then, few good images of names are available. Noted marine photographers such as the Rosenfelds amassed thousands of photographs of pleasure and racing yachts, yet their focus was rarely the stern. Their goal was to show the vessel in its most powerful or beautiful way, which usually meant a photo taken from the side or ahead.

Trade statistics show a spike in the growth of pleasure boating in the United States from the late 1940s into the mid-1950s, from over two million boats to nearly six million. This corresponded with the postwar surge in prosperity. Books such as *Chapman's Piloting, Seamanship and Small Boat Handling,* first published in 1923, were consistently updated to stay current with safety guidelines and government regulations, which evolved to keep pace with the surge.

Still, boat names remained mostly conventional at midcentury, both in name and design. The *Lloyd's Register* from 1950 includes fifty-five yachts using the word "wind," thirty using "white," and only a few offbeat names such as *What's Doin* and *Who Dat,* both of which appeared on boats under 35 feet. One of the noted fads of the time—but one that failed to make its way onto many of the yachts listed in *Lloyd's*—was stitching a name together Frankenstein fashion from parts of several family members' names. *KimBaBo* and the like were products of the trend toward more affordable and democratic boating—an activity that encouraged family participation—as opposed to yachting, which had been the exclusive domain of wealthy men. A *Time* magazine article of 1959 called this trend "Boat Fever."

Considering the proliferation of boating periodicals and the recognition of boating by mainstream media, there were surprisingly few articles about naming by midcentury. *Rudder, MotorBoating,* and *Yachting* occasionally featured articles on how to paint, apply, or maintain a name, but these did not explore the artistic or conceptual aspects of naming. The best place to find interesting lettering designs was in the trade magazines *Signs of the Times* and *Signcraft,* whose readership included sign painters and boat letterers who sent in examples of their handiwork. These examples showed some adventurousness and variety of design—with new script faces, swashes, outlines, and shadows—although the overall effect was still traditional. A large number of small, affordable boats were lettered directly by their owners. There was enough how-to information available, and anyone with a do-it-yourself inclination needed just a few simple tools. Only the occasional DIYer, however, was inclined to flex his or her creative muscle by using lowercase letterforms or atypical alignments or colors.

BREAKING WITH TRADITION

This brief look backward suggests that, for a span of over three thousand years, boat names were relatively consistent. Differences in the naming of warships and merchant ships and preferences for gender articles or for proper names versus honorary names make interesting maritime historical footnotes, but names were confined to a narrow spectrum of possibilities. And when they appeared on ships at all, they were rendered traditionally—usually in all capital serif lettering with a straight or an arched baseline.

By the 1950s, boating was a family activity. *Yachting* magazine's 1957 cover both encourages and pokes fun at do-it-yourself boatowners. There also may be two small jokes in the names themselves—*Quest* painted on a sailboat and *Utter Confusion* on a powerboat—along with the notion that many small outboard motorboats lacked names.

April, 1957
50 Cents

Yachting
POWER AND SAIL

UTTER

CONFUSION

Lois Darling

PRACTICAL HINTS ON "FITTING OUT"

LIGHT ON THE SAILCLOTH QUESTION ☆ FITTING OUT AN AMPHIBIOUS FLEET

SO YOU WANT TO PLANE?

Naming a boat is a challenge that rarely leaves a skipper at a loss. Punsters proliferate, outdoing one another with adroitly nautical wordplays like Wide A Wake (center) or the double-barreled Seaduced Too (upper right). Exotic lettering, such as the journalistic typeface on Bad News at center, offers further opportunities for some wit. Dinghies often receive affectionate diminutives or may derive their names even more directly from the mother vessel, as in the case of the fishing trawler and baby at lower right.

This spread from Time-Life's *Library of Boating* is truly representative of the variety of typefaces, goofy names, and uses of graphics employed by the mid-1970s.

By 1975, *Lloyd's Register* was showing a noticeable upgrade in the variety of names and their ingenuity. There were still plenty of names starting with "lady" or "miss," and many others that included "black" or "blue." And names beginning with "sea" continued their popularity. But these were accompanied by a larger admixture of offbeat names, many referencing pop culture. *Peyton's Place, 12th of Never,* and *Spicy Meatball* made their first appearances in *Lloyd's,* along with *Debt, Dry Martini, Shutterbug, Yes Dear, Y Worry,* and others.

This shift to humorous and personal names did not go unnoticed by more traditional sensibilities. In the mid-1970s L. Francis Herreshoff, a respected yacht designer, was prompted to write a piece for *Rudder* magazine (also included in his *Herreshoff Reader,* published in 1978) directly addressing boat names. He took a romantic view, insisting that American yachts were lacking in melodious names. He encouraged readers to use names that "have a pleasant sound" and conjure "pleasant thoughts," and to follow the tradition of naming boats after females. Names from the Spanish, Italian, and French languages struck him as particularly beautiful. He said that "the name of a yacht often very much affects her whole prestige; at times it even affects her value, or sales price, and even a beautiful yacht can be made to seem less beautiful if one associates an unbecoming name with her." He supplied his readers with a list of over 350 suggested names, mainly from mythology and his memories of past ships. *Angelica, Cygnet, Electra, Frolic, Galatea, Harmonia, Medea, Persephone, Selene, Thalia, Valhalla,* and *Zephyr* were all included.

In addition to resale value, Herreshoff offered other practical arguments to support his preferences. He believed, for example, that a melodious name such as *North Star* was more easily pronounced, recognized, and remembered—and therefore important for the safety of the crew should assistance be needed. "Trick names, ego names and rubber stamp names" were to be avoided because trick names required too much explanation, ego names showed a lack of romance and poetry, and rubber stamp names, in which an owner used the same name for each subsequent boat, were simply too confusing.

His true concern, however, was aesthetic. He went so far as to profess fear for the prestige of American yachting. Yachting—the domain of the wealthy—was undergoing a democratic transformation into boating—the domain of middle-class families. The genie was out of the bottle, spurred on not only by postwar prosperity but by the advent in the 1960s of fiberglass boats. (Elsewhere, Herreshoff famously dismissed fiberglass as "frozen snot.") For the first time multiple copies of a boat could be produced from a single mold, and boat prices fell in response. Democratic ownership trends unleashed a democratic profusion of naming preferences. Herreshoff's recommendations were the voice of tradition at a time in which names were breaking with it. Nowhere in the article did he make any suggestions for the design of a name, but it is safe to assume that his preference was classic serif lettering in all capital letters, or maybe a simple script.

By the 1980s boat naming was entirely in tune with popular culture and self-referential in a way that went against all of Herreshoff's ideas. Because names were creatively expanding, or perhaps because of their perceived brashness, more articles and experts offered suggestions, and naming books (akin to baby-naming books) were published for those in need of inspiration. In the *Practical Sailor Library* series of 1988, the editors added their voices in a chapter entitled "A Proper Name for a Proper Yacht." They took boaters to task over past excesses and a lack of creativity in names. They also lamented some of the earlier fads mentioned by Herreshoff, such as combination names and the use by the owner of the same name with a Roman numeral after it to designate sequentially owned boats. "Cute" names and names used by too many (*Spindrift, Mistral,* and *Typhoon* were mentioned) were also criticized as "group-think fixations." As a remedy they offered ground rules on naming, which included limiting the use of "see," "sea," or "C"; avoiding names that would attract law enforcement; and eliminating the use of the owner's name or profession (spelled backward, forward, or in any other clever permutation). The editors stated that the best names were pleasant-sounding ones that might be found in foreign or geographic references. Alternatively, they suggested that the owner should select a word that best described his feelings about the experience of boating or about the boat itself. A final bit of advice focused on how to display the chosen name, with a short description of custom versus off-the-shelf lettering.

By the late 1980s *Lloyd's Register* included more than three thousand names, and the number of nontraditional names continued to grow. In addition to a heavy dose of double entendres and pop culture references, more names focused on the owner's profession or successes, despite *Practical Sailor's* advice to the contrary. There were still plenty of boats using the words "blue," "black," or "wind" in the name, and names using "sea" represented over 10 percent of the list. Monikers such as *Big Mac Attack, Bilbo Baggins, Blade Runner,* and *My Three Sons* were trumped in other cases by the egos of owners, many of whom were riding the stock market and technology booms. Three boats simply called *Wall Street,* two called *Boardroom,* and others named *Bonus Check, Cash Flow, Cyber Cruiser II, Frozen Assets, HMS Software, Bald Ego, Fringe Benefits,* and *The Offish* were clear in their pride. Although the completely blunt *Phyl "T" Rich,* owned by Phyllis T. Toncray, combined in one name all the execrable tendencies identified by the *Practical Sailor* editors, ironically her boat was only a 36-footer.

It wasn't just Wall Streeters who subscribed to professional proclamations. The medical field was represented with *Dr. Feelgood, Suture Fancy, Suture Self,* and *3 Scalpels.* Other professions were represented in *Reel Tors, Sabbatical, Legal Tender, Fir Trader,* and *Bankers Choice.* Driven by a good economy, annual retail sales in the boating industry increased by more than five billion dollars between 1980 and 1985, and the number of pleasure craft in the United States topped 13,900,000.

Outlines, dropshadows, display typefaces, and multicolored graphics, so commonly available today in vinyl, were often still painted until the early 1990s.
All of the above are hand-painted.

WHY AQUAHOLIC?

In the last fifteen years names have continued to express the joy, cost, excitement, pleasure, and status associated with recreational boating and boatowners. A simple Internet search will lead you to a profusion of boat names and a great variety of visual examples of names displayed on boats. Since 1991 *Boating World* magazine has printed a list

of its Top Ten boat names for the year that derives from BoatUS.com's list of its most requested boat graphics. *Aquaholic* has been in the top ten since 2002, and *Seas the Day* is a current favorite. *Destiny* and *Serenity* are perennial favorites. Names such as *Island Time, Happy Hours, Osprey,* and *Wet Dream* move up and down on the list, suggesting that names really haven't varied significantly in the last fifteen years. Like *Lloyd's Register,* BoatUS.com's boat graphics aren't representative of all eighteen million-plus boats in the United States (with several times that number in the world as a whole), yet they do give a good sense of general trends.

Two other naming tendencies of the last fifteen years stand out. The first is that boats with nontraditional names are typically less than 50 feet long. The larger the boat, broadly speaking, the more traditional its name. For example, in a 2006 *Forbes* article about billionaires and the sizes of their yachts, the three largest yachts, ranging from 453 feet down to 377 feet, were named *Rising Sun, Octopus,* and *Alexander,* respectively. Names based on wordplay and double entendres are most commonly found on sportfishing boats under 32 feet.

The second tendency is that sailboats, regardless of size, have more traditional names than powerboats. Their names are more apt to refer to the sailing experience than the owner's profession or prowess.

AQUAHOLICS

The wind is an obvious, powerful theme for sailors in the same way that the pursuit of a quarry is for fishermen. Perhaps because sailors are more physically involved with their boats, they tend to cultivate a stronger tie to traditional aspects of the elements and the experience.

If you have difficulty settling on a name, take comfort that in a 2005 *Sports Illustrated* online survey, 22 percent of boaters said that coming up with a name for their boat was harder than naming their children or pets. In 2004 *Boating World* magazine asked its audience of small-powerboat owners how they had come up with a name. In reply, 30.9 percent of respondents said that the name referred to a family member or the family's last name; 27.6 percent said it referred to drinking or sex; 23 percent cited relaxation; 7 percent cited the boat's costs; 6.6 percent said the name referred to how hard they worked; and 4.9 percent chose a name that expressed patriotism.

A noteworthy change to naming comes from the commercial sphere. *Lloyd's List* decided to neuter its listings for commercial vessels and no longer refers to a ship as "she" in an effort to be more egalitarian and inoffensive to women. As we have seen in this brief naming history, pleasure boating in the past has taken its cues from military and merchant ships. Could your "she" become a "he" or an "it" in the future?

KING OF BOATS

AQUAHOLIC

These examples of *Aquaholic* were created by designers to show new solutions to a well-used name.

GONE FISSION

Having traced the history of boat naming from Egyptian god-kings into contemporary pop culture, it seems appropriate to end with an excursion into fictional ship names from modern literature, film, and television. Predictably, most such names follow tradition; there are the expected female names, references to mythology, and names after animals and birds. A few break the mold, however, and one among them that perfectly fits the current penchant for jokes and double entendres is *Gone Fission,* Mr. Burns's yacht on the television cartoon *The Simpsons.* The name of course references the nuclear power plant at which Homer Simpson works for Mr. Burns, and it has the added benefit of creating a good fishing joke. The show's appearance in the late 1980s dovetails perfectly with the name chosen. It's goofy, and it makes a statement about the owner's professional life.

Two names that may have been a little ahead of their time were *We're Here,* from Rudyard Kipling's 1897 novel *Captains Courageous,* and *Wonkatania,* from Willy Wonka & the Chocolate Factory in 1971. *We're Here,* the fictional New England fishing vessel, seems an unconventional choice given the taciturn reputation of New England fishermen. *Wonkatania* combines Wonka with a suffix associated with such giant vessels as the *Lusitania* (a passenger ship that was sunk by a German submarine) and *Mauritania* (an early 1900s immigrant ship) to humorous effect.

Among the best-known fictional names is the *SS Minnow* from the 1960s television show *Gilligan's Island.* As the story goes, the name was an intentional insult to the chairman of the FCC, Newton Minow, whom *Gilligan's Island* producer Sherwood Schwartz felt was giving too much programming authority to the networks to the detriment of television shows. The beached boat was a metaphor for this sentiment. The use of the prefix "SS," meaning steamship, for a small boat powered by a diesel engine was another interesting choice. In part it may have been a nod to Schwartz's initials, but it also lampooned the skipper's (and by extension Minow's) pretentiousness. Four different boats were used over the run of the series, but it appears that the name was consistently hand-lettered in sans serif capital letters on a nameboard attached to the bow.

Other notable fictional names include the *Black Pearl* (from the *Pirates of the Caribbean* films), *Demeter* (from Bram Stoker's novel *Dracula*), *Hispaniola* (from the Robert Louis Stevenson classic *Treasure Island*), *Nautilus* (from Jules Verne's *Twenty Thousand Leagues Under the Sea*), *Pequod* (from Herman Melville's masterpiece, *Moby-Dick*), and the name to top all names, *SS More Powerful than Superman, Batman, Spiderman, and the Incredible Hulk Put Together,* from the *Family Guy* animated television series.

a letterer's story

Carla Christopher
BoatArt.com, Fort Lauderdale, Florida

STAYING AFLOAT

In the early days of computer technology, before making the transition from hand painting, Carla Christopher found herself "getting buried" by the vinyl lettering shops. Not yet ready to buy her own equipment, but wanting to provide vinyl names to her customers, Carla subcontracted the production of some of her artwork to the shops.

Then a customer requested something unique for his boat *Ali Kat*. Carla suggested ideas such as painting a cat here or cat eyes there, but the customer wasn't taken with these approaches.

Thus challenged, Carla decided to forget what was typical to do in paint and push at what might be possible in vinyl. Now she describes it as a pivotal experience. The concept she wanted to portray was a cat moving in the background of the letters just as an alley cat might slink behind trash cans.

Carla drew a sketch in heavy black marker, marked it up to show what image areas she wanted green or white, and faxed it to her vinyl subcontractor. The large areas of color suited the capabilities of

early cut vinyl technology, and Carla's inventive use of negative and positive (white and green) spaces integrated the name and image in a novel fashion.

The boatowner loved it—in fact, he went nuts. And Carla said, "The clouds parted for me. I wasn't scared to be experimental or creative when using vinyl anymore."

Today Carla and her employees work with sophisticated technology. One of her favorite lettering stories involves a 90-foot boat with a teak transom and the name *Reel Money*.

Reel Money's owner was a boat broker who had just done a major overhaul on the yacht. He was ready to sell it and wanted a boat-name design that would attract attention. Having worked with Carla in the past, he gave her free reign. Carla took advantage of the opportunity to develop something complex and fun, even though she was working with common fishing motifs.

Using technology to its fullest, Carla set the name in 22 karat engine-turned vinyl letters with a black outline that was selectively shadowed in gray for added dimension. The image elements were beautifully integrated—the fish believably swimming out of the "M," the fishing line wrapping

"Reel," and the fishing rod tucked into the descender of the "y" all felt carefully considered. The rod's position at the crook of the "y" nearly personified it by insinuating that it was an arm. And subtler elements were there too. The money used as bait was in the denomination of three million dollars and sported the Statue of Liberty in the oval.

The *Reel Money* name was unfortunately short-lived because the yacht was purchased and renamed *Captain Jack*. The good news for Carla was that she was hired to design that name too. For *Captain Jack,* Carla paired a stylized typeface, which captured an old-time spirit, with a weapon-toting one-eyed pirate who demanded to be taken seriously. The finishing touch was the hailing port, which looked as if it had been written on a parchment scroll or carved into a nameboard. A simple color palette worked with the teak transom and kept the design's diverse elements from becoming too busy.

Sadly, the end of this tale isn't as lovely as the design. *Captain Jack* was shipwrecked after only a short time on the water. Superstitious mariners hold that it's bad luck to change the name of a boat…but that never stops anyone!

a letterer's story

Lisa Hutchinson
Daydream Designs, Beverly, Massachusetts

YOUNG DREAMERS

A teacher, a fireman, and a psychologist walk into a bar.

No, this isn't a joke. The teacher, the fireman, and the psychologist were three young men in their early twenties, and it wasn't a bar they walked into but Lisa Hutchinson's sign shop. The three men had purchased their used sailboat in Beverly and needed an artful design for their chosen name, *La Cucaracha.* Lisa had been recommended.

All three were from Norway and had decided to sail around the world. It was a crazy dream, especially considering that one of them didn't even know how to sail, but they were hoping that their passion for "the tour" would compensate for their lack of experience.

They warned Lisa that they were on a limited budget because all their money was committed to the trip. A very simple vinyl name was all they could afford.

Lisa met with them and loved their spirit and enthusiasm. She also loved the name of their boat. For the owners, the cockroach represented

tenacity, adaptability, and peskiness—and of course the ability to survive anything.

Lisa suggested that an oblique (slanted to the right) typeface might look good and create a sense of motion, and the three men agreed. They were living on the boat and had no access to a fax or computer, so after preparing several options Lisa drove to the marina. The men liked so many of her concepts that they decided to sleep on it. The next day they called with their decision.

The design they liked wasn't Lisa's first choice, though she felt it captured the essence of the name. The sharp and angular edges represent a cockroach's legs, and the simple highlight and dark shadow add dimension. You can almost imagine the space between the name and the black shadow being a perfect crevice for la cucaracha to crawl into, and the position of the cockroach on the transom suggests that it might be heading that way.

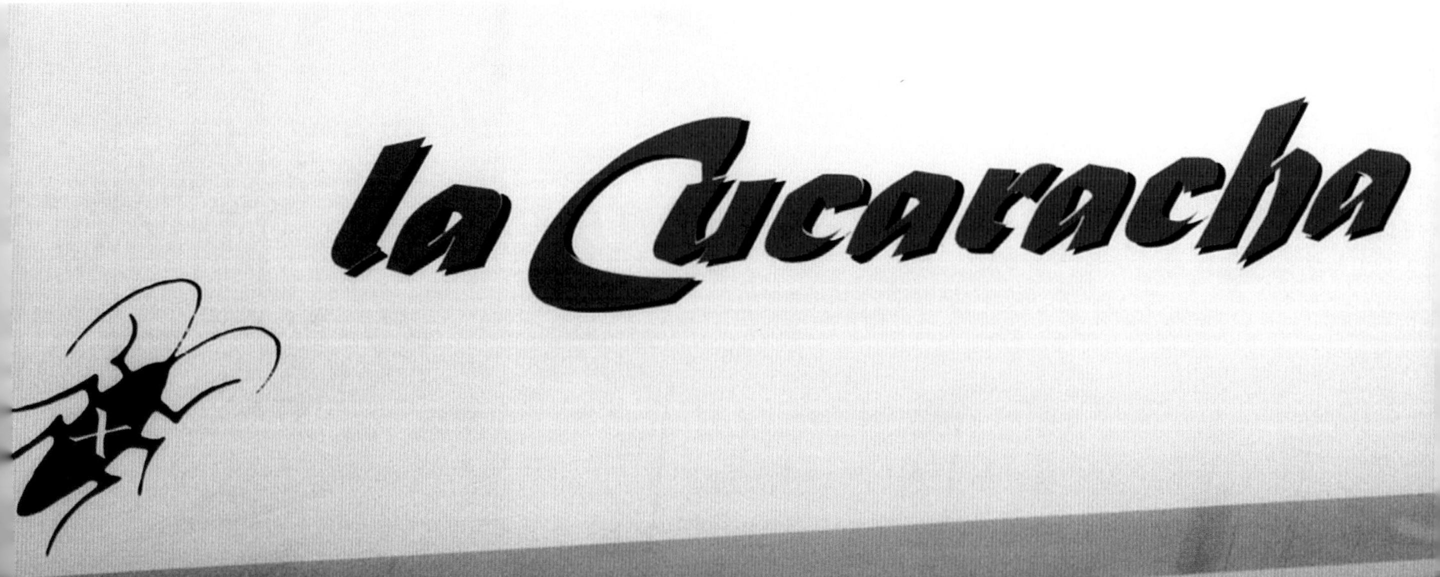
la Cucaracha

Passion for boating can be expressed in both the name and design—when you love it, let everyone know. Don't settle for the predictable. *Spoiled* sports an expressive script appropriately finished in silver leaf, a notoriously expensive and pesky material. *Dynamite* is hand-painted utilizing a fun graphic that substitutes for the "I" and overlapping off-kilter letters that emphasize volatility. *Easy Street* beautifully integrates an image and text into a unit that tells the whole story without being literal.

love

A BOMB · ABOVE AND BEYOND · ACCLAIM · ACE · ADDICT · ADORABLE · AGLO · ALL JOY · ALL OUT · ALLURE · AMAZING · AMBROSIA ·

AWE · BEAUTIFUL · BED OF ROSES · BELLY RUB · BEST LOVE · BETA · BEWITCHED · BIG DEAL · BIG TIME · BLAZE OF GLORY · BLIND

REASON · BLISS · BODACIOUS · BODY AND SOUL · BONUS · BRASS TACKS · BRAVO · BREATHLESS · CAKE WALK · CAMELOT · CANDY ·

CARROT · CASTLE · CAT'S PAJAMAS · CAVORT · CHAMPAGNE · CHARISMA · CHARMER · CHEERS · CHERRY BOMB · COMPELLING ·

CONTAGIOUS · CRAZY · DAILY DOUBLE · DARLING · DASHING · DELIGHT · DELIRIOUS · DREAM BOAT · EAGER · EASY · ECSTATIC ·

ENAMOR · ENCHANTED · ENJOY · EPIC · EUPHORIA · FANATIC · FANCY FREE · FANDANGO · FANTASEA · FASCINATION · FAWN ·

FELICITY · FETCHING · FEVERISH · FINE FETTLE · FLAIR · FLAUNT · FREE WILL · FROLIC · FULL THROTTLE · GA GA · GAIETY · GIDDY ·

ELIXIR

ALTER EGO

HELL YEAH!

Can't

ASPIRATION

B HA

KISMET

NO

GLEE · GOLDEN · GOOD LIFE · GOODNESS · GOOSE BUMPS · GORGEOUS · GUSTO · HAPPY · HEAVEN · HOME RUN ·

HOORAY · HUZZAH · INCREDIBLE · IRRESISTIBLE · JOY · JUBILATION · KING · LARK · LOOPY · LOVABLE · LOVE ·

LUCKY · MAGIC · MARVEL · MECCA · MERRY · MUCHO MAS · NO LIMITS · OGLE · OUT OF SIGHT · OVERJOYED · PASSION ·

PAY DIRT · PLUCKY · POT OF GOLD · PRIZE · QUIVER · RADIANCE · RAPTURE · SERUM · SLAP HAPPY · SUPER DUPER ·

TERRIFIC · ULTIMATE · ULTRA · UTMOST · WONDEROUS · YAHOO · XOXOXOX

Fuggedaboudit

Waite

Bodacious

Dev Ocean

Sweet

Free Spirit
GREENWICH, CT

RULES

DESTINY

and passion

Enthusiasm sometimes demands attention.
Bold type, bouncing baselines, and display
typefaces offer ways to express your name's
meaning. Punctuation and well-placed
graphics also add interest if not overdone.

chapter two
FINDING YOUR STYLE

For centuries the styling of boat names was simple and formal.

Hand-painted letters met the needs of working and military boatowners

who were required to show a name on the hull of their boats. Serif or

sans serif capital letters were two of the most common styles, with

upper- and lowercase script letters making up the third. The straight

forward lettering mirrored the classic styles used in commercial

advertisements and promotions up through the mid-nineteenth century.

Boat lettering was (and still is) a style follower, not a trendsetter.

Throughout the twentieth century, as advertising and popular culture

experimented with more expressive typography, imagery, and brands,

boat lettering followed behind, sometimes slowly.

LETTERING THROUGH THE 1960S

The turn of the twentieth century brought the first real wave of affordable pleasure boats and a proliferation of new type designs to the United States. Still, boat lettering continued to hark back to the utilitarian styles used on working boats. This was due in part to function and tradition, but also to the skills and training of boat letterers.

Boat lettering might be learned through schooling or an apprenticeship but was just as often self-taught from one of the many sign-painting or lettering how-to books available in the early 1900s. Many such books based their guidance on the author's own experiences or interests, each promoting his or her approach as the "proper" one. Nearly all the books shared two ideas, however. One was that lettering was an art form and as such encouraged individualism —though not at the expense of legibility; the second was that good craftsmanship could nevertheless be easily distinguished from bad. To learn the trade of good lettering, a student needed diligence, a command of the tools, and an eye for understanding letterforms both alone and in relationship to one another. Skillful execution of a lettering style came only from hours of practicing strokes with a pen or brush.

Four styles commonly employed by boat letterers were roman, gothic, italic, and script—roman being defined by books of the time as anything serifed, gothic as anything of relatively uniform width without serifs, italic as anything slanted, and script as anything with connected letterforms. Some letterers and books subdivided scripts into formal and informal (also known as brush, or casual) scripts. To add to the confusion, the gothic style was also referred to as Egyptian or block depending on a letterer's schooling or experience. To one letterer gothic meant a sans serif as described here, and to another it meant a style modeled after Germanic letterforms of the Middle Ages.

By far the most common configuration on a transom featured the boat name in roman or gothic capital letters with the hailing port centered directly below it in gothic capitals. The visual interplay between name and hailing port resembled a headline and subhead in advertising text, with the boat name being larger than the hailing port to create a hierarchy. The name/hailing port unit would be sized to center comfortably on the transom. On boats with limited transom space or uniquely styled hulls, the name might appear instead on the bow or pilothouse.

Pages from lettering books demonstrate various styles and the names given those styles. Such guides were used both for professional instruction and by laypeople interested in learning hand lettering alphabets and techniques.

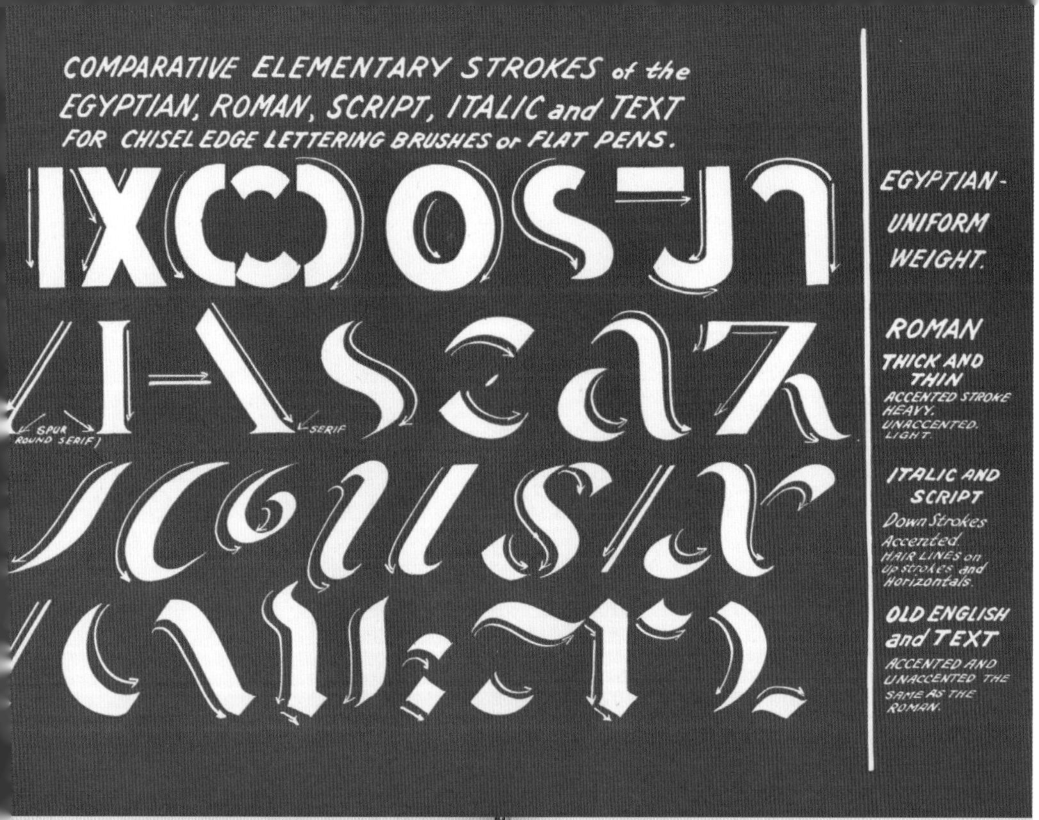

COMPARATIVE ELEMENTARY STROKES of the
EGYPTIAN, ROMAN, SCRIPT, ITALIC and TEXT
FOR CHISEL EDGE LETTERING BRUSHES or FLAT PENS.
SPUR
ROUND SERIF)
SERIF
EGYPTIAN -
UNIFORM
WEIGHT.
ROMAN
THICK AND
THIN
ACCENTED STROKE
HEAVY.
UNACCENTED.
LIGHT.
ITALIC AND
SCRIPT
Down Strokes
Accented.
HAIR LINES on
up strokes and
Horizontals.
OLD ENGLISH
and TEXT
ACCENTED AND
UNACCENTED THE
SAME AS THE
ROMAN.

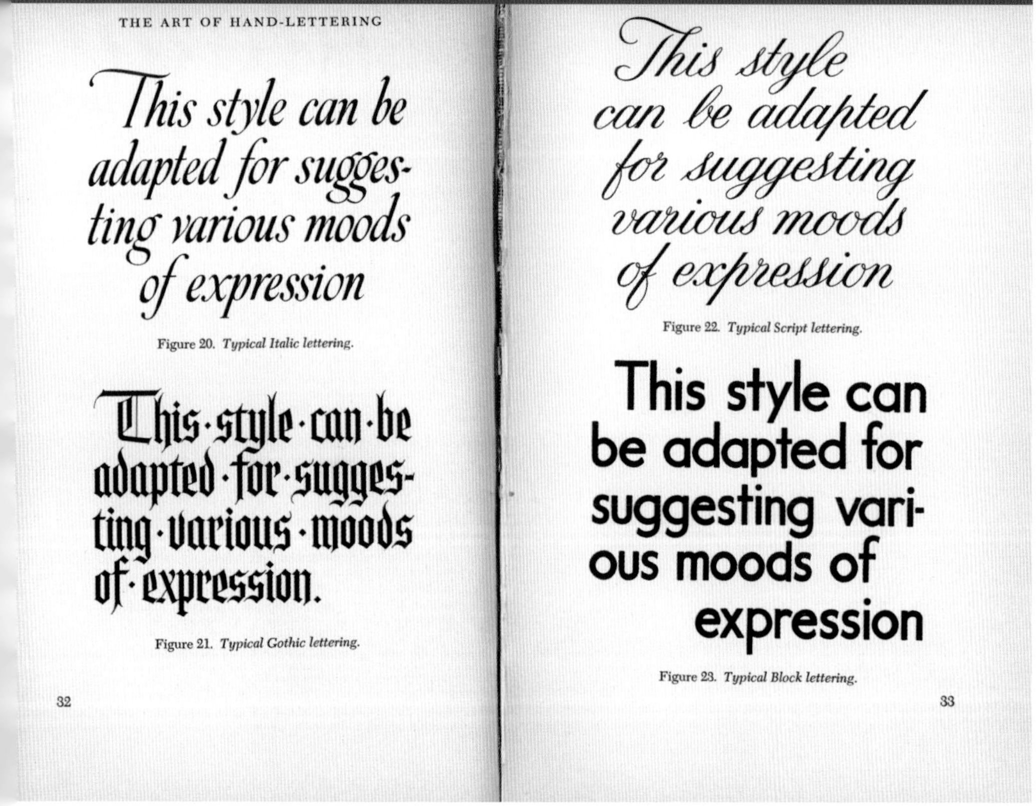

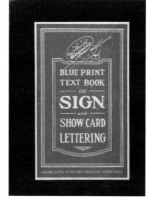

THE ART OF HAND-LETTERING

This style can be adapted for sugges-ting various moods of expression

Figure 20. *Typical Italic lettering.*

This·style·can·be adapted·for·sugges-ting·various·moods of·expression.

Figure 21. *Typical Gothic lettering.*

32

This style can be adapted for suggesting various moods of expression

Figure 22. *Typical Script lettering.*

This style can be adapted for suggesting vari-ous moods of expression

Figure 23. *Typical Block lettering.*

33

BLUE PRINT
TEXT BOOK
OF
SIGN
and
SHOW CARD
LETTERING

THE
ART OF
HAND-
LETTER-
ING

Speedball
textbook
for pen & brush
lettering
18th edition

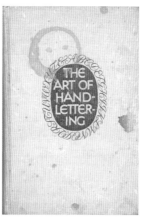

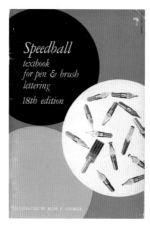

High Seas
High Seas
Garamond

High Seas
High Seas
Caslon

High Seas
High Seas
Bodoni

Villome

BARCHETTA

MARBLEHEAD

Lettering a boat name was similar to lettering a business name, and the conventions used by a sign painter for a shop window or door were commonly applied to boat names. Boat letterers for the most part were also sign painters, as few could maintain a business solely reliant on lettering boats. Their resultant emphasis on legibility and readability prompted traditional lettering treatments, with function trumping expression well into mid-1900s. Favored typefaces in the roman style—such as Garamond, Caslon, and Bodoni—were known to most letterers, and variations of them were widely used on boats. These type families were extremely common in printed matter and prominently featured in how-to lettering books because they had been available in set type for more than a century. Their variations of thick and thin strokes and upright or slanted stresses provided enough freedom for letterers to relate the style of a boat name to its meaning if desired.

Barchetta is a classic contemporary beauty for many reasons. The name, lettered in Caslon, incorporates ligatures (the joining of two letters as seen in "AR" and "TA"), good letterspacing, and a perfectly arched baseline that follows the transom shape. The letters are hand gold-leafed and outlined in black for emphasis against the wood. Painted detail lines add dimension and visual weight to the letters, and the name and hailing port are appropriately proportioned to each other and to the size of the transom.

Italic and script styles were considered classic too, though not painted as often as roman or gothic. Italics were generally modeled after the Garamond, Caslon, or Bodoni italics and were used to represent action or speed for a boat name such as *High Seas*. Scripts were favored for more feminine names, and an oversize script letter (or in some typefaces available as swash capitals or alternate glyphs) would commonly begin a name, while a swash or flourish element might close it. This approach achieved a fancier or more flowing visual appearance. Combining scripts and italics produced designs that could reference the wind, the tides, or a journey in names such as *Windswept*, *Wave Dancer*, or *Tenacity*.

Just as traditional lettering styles predominated into the mid-twentieth century, the color palette used for boat names retained a small range too. Black, blue, and gold were the dominant colors. Boats with a light-colored transom typically used either a combination of black or dark blue letters with a gold outline; black or dark blue letters with a

Villomee and *Hyltonian* are examples of names that open with swash capital letters and use script typefaces. Scripts have connected letterforms but aren't always slanted, as in *Hyltonian* (which is also hand gold-leafed and outlined). *WindSong* is an italic typeface with a calligraphic oblique stress (right slant) and interesting finishing strokes such as the ascender of the "d" and the loop of the "g." All such subtle typographic nuances influence the distinctness of a name.

blue or gray dropshadow; or gold-leaf letters with a black outline. On boats with a darker transom, gold-leaf letters with black outlines were the standard presentation. The great popularity of blue, especially on light-colored transoms, stemmed from its association with water. Blue was also a popular accent color on boat exteriors for the same reason, and letterers sought to match the accent color to make the name seem a natural extension of the boat.

While most boat names were professionally hand-painted, other options were available for the industrious boatowner. He (or she) could try his own hand at painting or purchase ready-made letters. Companies such as Bernard Engraving Company of Toledo, Ohio, sold molded plastic letters and numbers along with their pressure-sensitive Super-Stik letters, the precursor to vinyl lettering. Known for their quality and readily available in marine shops, the company's products made it easy and inexpensive to adhere a name to a transom. Bernard's advertisements, which ran in *Yachting* magazine from the 1950s through the early 1970s, provide an accurate picture of the limited range of lettering options at that time. One ad asked, "Who offers a wider selection of letters and numbers than a Bernard Engraving dealer?" and then answered, "Nobody." Bernard proudly offered three lettering styles (Hi-Style Script, Classic Roman, and Gothic) in five sizes and four color combinations while encouraging owners to "give in to that creative urge." To further encourage that urge, Bernard introduced in 1974 solid white molded plastic letters and numbers that could be hand- or spray-painted in any color to suit the whim of the boatowner. Bernard Engraving, now headquartered in Bridgeport, Connecticut, continues to make letters, numbers, and a broad range of signage for the marine industry.

Although a midcentury boat letterer's repertoire of type styles and colors was small by today's standards, ingenuity and personal style were nevertheless evident in the work. A letterer's creativity expressed itself in the spacing, or kerning, of letters and in swash letters (letters with fancy tails or curled extensions), oversize letters, ornamental flourishes and underlines, interesting dimensional effects, and the integration of imagery with type. Creative compositions of letters were favored over pictorial elements to give visual expression to a name. Literal depictions such as a moon for the name *Moonglow* were atypical. Innovation was evident, but it was confined to a smaller range of typographic nuances than we associate with modern boat graphics.

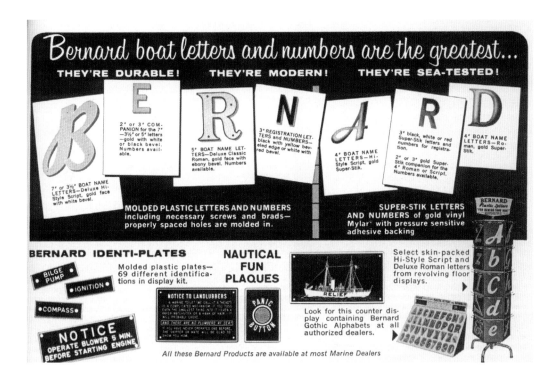

Bernard boat letters and numbers are the greatest...

THEY'RE DURABLE! THEY'RE MODERN! THEY'RE SEA-TESTED!

7" or 3½" BOAT NAME LETTERS—Deluxe Hi-Style Script, gold face with white bevel.

2" or 3" COMPANION for the 7"—3½" or 5" letters —gold with white or black bevel. Numbers available.

5" BOAT NAME LETTERS—Deluxe Classic Roman, gold face with ebony bevel. Numbers available.

3" REGISTRATION LETTERS and NUMBERS— black with yellow beveled edge or white with red bevel.

4" BOAT NAME LETTERS—Hi-Style Script, gold Super-Stik.

3" black, white or red Super-Stik letters and numbers for registration.

2" or 3" gold Super-Stik companion for the 4" Roman or Script. Numbers available.

4" BOAT NAME LETTERS—Roman, gold Super-Stik.

MOLDED PLASTIC LETTERS AND NUMBERS including necessary screws and brads— properly spaced holes are molded in.

SUPER-STIK LETTERS AND NUMBERS of gold vinyl Mylar² with pressure sensitive adhesive backing

BERNARD IDENTI-PLATES

BILGE PUMP
IGNITION
COMPASS
NOTICE OPERATE BLOWER 5 MIN. BEFORE STARTING ENGINE

Molded plastic plates— 69 different identifications in display kit.

NAUTICAL FUN PLAQUES

NOTICE TO LANDLUBBERS
PANIC BUTTON

Select skin-packed Hi-Style Script and Deluxe Roman letters from revolving floor displays.

Look for this counter display containing Bernard Gothic Alphabets at all authorized dealers.

All these Bernard Products are available at most Marine Dealers

COLOR ME BLUE
or GREEN ...
or SCREAMING YELLOW!

A new feature in the very popular Bernard line of Boat Numbers and Letters for 1974 are the solid white molded plastic alphabets for dark hulls that may be spray-painted any color you desire. Available in the 7" or 3½" Hi-Style Script, the 5" Classic Roman and matching Port of Hail Gothic letters. Suitable spray lacquers are available at most Marine Dealers.

May be painted with a brush or sprayed any color you desire!

Ask about the complete line of Bernard Boat Letters and Numbers, including the Bernard Identi-plates for instrument panels and the whimsical Bernard Fun Plaques.

Phone or Write for Complete Catalog

ENGRAVING
Bernard
COMPANY

5055 Stickney Ave., Toledo, Ohio 43612
Phone 419/729-3914

BUY YOUR LETTERS AT THE SIGN OF QUALITY

Bernard Engraving, a frequent advertiser in *Yachting* magazine, offered innovations in plastic letters and numbers.
(Top: *Yachting,* 1967; Bottom: *Yachting,* 1974)

In these more contemporary examples, practiced letter-ers took advantage of scale, spacing, and ornament when positioning individual letter-forms. The tail of the "R" cups the curve of the "S"below; decorative crossbars for the "A" and "E" in *Ragtime* add distinction; and in *No Fear*, the capitals "N" and "F" are reduced to almost the size of the lowercase letters to create visual flow.

Hand-painted boat names from this era are rare today, especially on seaworthy vessels. Occasionally a boatyard castoff with a shadow of a name can be found, and it is possible to see original brushstrokes. Beyond that, some working boats maintain their painted lettering, but ownership changes and vinyl lettering have pretty much banished mid-century painted lettering styles from pleasure boats.

THE ADVENT OF FREE-FORM LETTERING

Traditional lettering styles continued to dominate through the late 1960s, with boat size, model, location, powering method, or cost seeming to have little impact on the design of a name. The popular choice remained conventional all capital letters in a serif or maybe a sans serif type. It is hard to determine the precise point in the 1970s at which boat-name designs became more experimental, but it's possible to identify a couple of factors that influenced the shift.

First, in a backlash to the popular sans serif typography of 1950s advertising, new experimentation pushed type styles forward. Eclectic 1960s styles, including psychedelia and revivals, were applied to edgier cultural items such as records and magazines. The California custom car craze brought "Big Daddy" Roth's Rat Fink hot-rod character and his gang to the masses, and in 1968 the Mattel Company introduced a line of diecast custom toy cars called Hot Wheels (the company's answer to the popular Matchbox toy cars), featuring a wavy, groovy, hand-lettered logo that connoted speed, power, and fantasy. These new graphic art expressions found their way onto surfboards, into the pages of *Mad Magazine,* and elsewhere through popular culture, and soon boat lettering was following their lead. The names and graphics representing car culture, both toy and real, were dramatic. The first Hot Wheels models sported names such as Python and Hot Heap, and "Big Daddy" Roth's first car was called Little Jewel. These names were accompanied by highly stylized hand lettering that broke conventions, mixing capital and lowercase letters and allowing individual letterforms to bounce above and below the baseline.

Whereas the car culture used hand lettering, innovations in commercial typesetting, such as phototypesetting and Letraset press type, gave birth to whimsical and distorted typestyles including Baby Teeth and Hairpin. The almost pictorial quality of this type, and many more designed at the time, encouraged a new level of creativity and experimentation with letterforms. The adoption of wholly new typestyles into mainstream culture influenced boat letterers and their customers to consider more daringly designed names.

Coinciding with these innovations were personalized car vanity plates. Commonly available to any resident in most states by the late 1970s, car owners were challenged to create "shorthand" monikers and clever nicknames to express themselves. Often self-referential, these plates offered the same outward identification to other drivers as boat names did for other boaters. An interest in public personalization crossed over to possessions such as cars and vacation homes.

The second and probably more significant reason for more expressive boat-name designs was the postwar fiberglass revolution in boatbuilding. Sailboat builders were quick to move from wood to fiberglass, while powerboat builders made the shift more slowly, until by the late 1960s fiberglass boats significantly outnumbered wood. For the first time multiple copies of a boat could be produced from a single mold, and the prices of new boats fell substantially. The result, when coupled

Curvy, hand-drawn letters, inventive and large drop-shadows, and other embellishments were common elements of 1970s lettering.

with postwar prosperity, was a democratization of boating. Indeed, the very concept of boating—as opposed to "yachting"—moved into the mainstream for the first time. A half century before, when asked about the cost of yachting, J. Pierpont Morgan had famously replied, "If you have to ask, you can't afford it." That was no longer true of boating.

Fiberglass offered such savings in maintenance, repairs, and resale, as well as in purchase cost, that it seemed to unleash a new freedom in boat names too. According to Daniel Spurr, author of *Heart of Glass: Fiberglass Boats and the Men Who Built Them,* "The industry's fiberglass branch also became less conservative…More builders began splashing their boats with vibrant colors, accent stripes, and other graphic details that shook free the shackles of tradition, and embraced instead exuberant creativity."

Even though their tools remained low-tech, boat letterers embraced the spirit of change in construction, culture, and typography by painting more inventive boat names that incorporated imagery and played with text and image relationships. One advantage letterers enjoyed over commercial typesetters in the 1970s was the ease with which they could overlap, layer, and manipulate letters in a way that was still manually and technically cumbersome for typesetters. Popular consumer graphics featured these hand skills in freestyle illustrated artwork, driving up the general acceptance of looser and more figurative text, which then encouraged boat letterers to use more visually descriptive lettering styles in their work. Letterers collected thick reference files of typography and unique letterform samples to use as inspiration—and to manipulate in their own designs.

THE VINYL INVASION

The 1980s constituted a watershed decade for the boating industry. Money spent at the retail level for recreational boating nearly doubled, from 7.5 to 13 billion dollars, in the first five years of the decade. The boating economy found itself booming right alongside the U.S. economy, with more boaters, bigger boats, and greater consumer demand for boating accessories.

Some of this demand was met by the introduction of vinyl technology for making boat letters. Vinyl capability established new standards that reflected the prosperity of the times and caught up boat lettering with the fiberglass boat revolution as well as with popular design trends.

Vinyl technology brought a new visual and typographic language to boat names. Simple names in simple lettering seemed too plain for boats by the late 1980s. Vinyl letters also had an interesting effect on those letterers who were still hand painting. The competition encouraged them to develop more complicated designs that could do things not yet possible in vinyl. Carla Christopher's *Dragon Lady,* for example, was a complex painting in which detailed, colorful imagery and stylized text were carefully integrated. Its multiple layering of colors, text, and image would have been difficult to achieve in the early days of vinyl because vinyl didn't layer successfully.

Few owners take advantage of their boat's full transom for the name. *Dragon Lady* was carefully designed to leverage all of the space and finds just the right visual balance between name and illustration.

Handlettered, *Sorciere*, *Nautica*, *Rowena*, and *Mama's Money* feature elements distinctive to the letterer's hand. *Sorciere*'s swash "S," calligraphic strokes, and underline all support the name's meaning. *Nautica* has an atypical backslant and utilizes swash elements to frame individual letterforms. *Rowena*'s letterforms are a nod to Mistral and incorporate highlights that add dimension and appear neon-like. And *Mama's Money*'s condensed letters, heavy shadow, and swashes are noticeably quirky.

Boat names themselves became more inspired, sometimes humorous and sometimes intimating the desires or circumstances of their owners. Names such as *Toucan Go, Got Time?, Sea Renity Now,* and *Halcyon Daze* suggested retirees out cruising. *Party of Five* and *Daddy's Cat* were probably family boats. *Bite Me, Four Reel,* and *Gone Fishing* belonged to sportfishing enthusiasts. And *Fowl Doc, Sea Surgeon,* and *Scoolie* hinted at their owners' occupations. Clever names, double entendres, and puns abounded, with words such as "reel," "sea," and "knot" appropriated for all kinds of meanings.

Other design trends were notable in the 1980s. While the use of blue had long been favored for names and pinstriping, a combination of dark blue letters with a light blue or gray shadow became the predictable standard. The prominence of blue can be attributed in part to the limited palette of vinyl colors available then. Teal, another favorite shade of blue, mirrored television shows such as *Miami Vice* and the design style known as Memphis, which liberally employed a palette of playful colors including teal and pink. Never a leader, boat lettering continued to follow the popular styles.

Some fonts were trendy too. As boat letterer Cindy Fletcher-Holden of Annapolis, Maryland, remembers, "Brush Script was so overdone in the '80s. It got to the point that, when people requested Brush Script, I'd suggest we pick something else." Other typefaces, such as Clarendon and Mistral, were popular to the point of overuse as well. The stylized letterforms of scripts such as Brush and Mistral probably struck boaters as fresh and evocative of the spirit of the water. The textured edges of Mistral, in particular, made letterforms appear almost wet. Additionally, such scripts suggested free-form handwriting in a time when ever fewer boats had their names painted by hand, so they had a "bad boy" appeal—much like similar typefaces on the products of such surf and watersport companies as Ocean Pacific and Quicksilver.

Mistral

Modeled after his own handwriting, Mistral was designed by Roger Excoffon in 1953.

Brush Script

Brush Script was designed by Robert E. Smith in 1942.

From the 1990s forward, boat graphics have continued to become more innovative, utilizing an almost endless variety of concepts, fonts, and artwork. Boat names have developed a distinctive brand of creative, visual identifiers that imbue a vessel with immediate personality. Viewed from a dock or marina, the design of a boat's name can instantly conjure some insight about the boat and its owner. The complete adoption of digital technology by boat graphics companies, an improved visual literacy among the boating public, and a focus on design and branding in popular culture are all contributing to the creative expression of boat names.

Digital vinyl technology has almost completely replaced hand painting. Among the limited number of remaining letterers, many of whom own their own digital sign shops, are some who still love to use their brushes when possible. Lisa Hutchinson, of Daydream Designs in Beverly, Massachusetts, prefers to hand letter whenever she can. "It just looks more creative," she says. "Tiny imperfections give hand lettering a unique appeal, and you can create letter styles that nobody has seen before. Hand lettering just has a little more creative flow to it."

While styles have certainly evolved, and many boat-name designs reflect the visual complexity of popular culture, traditional styling has by no means gone out of style. There are still plenty of boatowners who regard a classic serif typeface in capital letters as the perfect expression of their boat's spirit. Just as some upscale retailers often have the simplest logos and brands, simplicity and complexity both have their place on boats.

Ironically, even as advances in boat graphics have contributed exciting designs, advances in the design of boat sterns have forfeited space for those graphics. Responding to the times and their customers' desires, boat designers have exchanged the broad, uncluttered transoms of yesteryear for engine room doors, gear lockers, swim platforms, and more recreational space. The loser in the redesign can be the boat name. It has to either be scaled to fit a smaller space or moved to another place on the hull.

FINDING YOUR STYLE

With nearly limitless creative options, how do you develop a design for your boat's name that communicates what you want it to? Especially in our design-, brand-, and trend-conscious culture, we want to make a meaningful choice. Our boats can express status, taste, ego, or values just as our cars or houses can—perhaps more. Your boat's name, the final touch before it "splashes," will remain an outward visual signifier until it is removed.

Some design preferences seem to depend on the length of a boat— these are noted here *not* as a prescription but by way of background. Small to medium-size power- and sailboats—ranging from less than 20 to roughly 65 feet—tend to have the most playful names and associated graphics. Owners of these boats create the graphics themselves or work with a designer. Yachts 65 feet or more long, and especially megayachts (generally considered yachts more than 100 feet long, though that threshold is rising with the tide of the world's megamillionaires), favor more traditional styling, and often the professional captain or the broker of the boat will be responsible for hiring out the

WHY TIMES (NEW) ROMAN?

Although argued by some type historians, the most accepted history of Times New Roman has it designed by Victor Lardent for Stanley Morison in 1931. Originally developed as the typeface for the *London Times* newspaper, it has been redrawn multiple times and issued digitally by different type foundries as either Times Roman, Times New Roman, or simply Times, each with subtle differences.

Not until the advent of vinyl letters did the Times New Roman family of type replace Garamond and Caslon. Today, Times New Roman is one of the most proffered serif typefaces on font menus for boat graphics companies, while Garamond and Caslon may not even appear. One of the simplest reasons for the shift is the ubiquitous nature of the font once it became available on any personal computer or boat graphics system. From that point it has been recognized as a universal example of the roman style, and many members of the boating public ask for it by name.

MY BOAT NAME in Times *(Apple computer's version of Times)*

design. Sportfishing boats, racing boats, and muscle boats occupy a category of their own. At almost any size they have adventurous names and graphics, and many have artwork that wraps the entire boat—the seagoing equivalent of full-body tattoos.

Small boats feature some of the most lively graphics—goofy names, exaggerated typefaces, and caricatures galore—expressions of the pure pleasure the boats provide their owners. Some owners, not tied to tradition, choose to make humorous statements about their fishing success, marital status, or work ethic in their name choices. *Toy Box*, a powerboat hailing from Commerce, Michigan, embodies this idea. The design by Renee Anderson, of Signs by Renee, in Marathon, Florida, includes a cartoon-style typeface in which every letter is a different color along with a humorous illustration of a person bent over a trunk pulling out all kinds of fishing gear.

The playfulness and complexity of these illustrations have been made easier using digital technology and better through customization. Bold and bright, each graphic humorously visualizes the name, and by its detail, gives more backstory to the meaning of the name. This whimsical approach to a name is more commonly seen on smaller boats. *Fire Fly* is notable for its well-positioned stacked type and *Stray Dog*'s typestyle is a good match for the line weight used in the dog illustration.

Owners of medium-size to large boats are often involved in every aspect of their boat's purchase or design, building, and upkeep. Such a boat is likely to be the most valued and perhaps most costly possession of its owner. These owners may want to have fun with their boat's name, but because their investment of time and money is great, their consideration of the graphics may be too. Names and styles among these boats have the broadest range. There are traditional female and mythological names set off in formal lettering and standard colors, or statements such as *Flying Low* that intimate an owner's profession with a display type and supporting graphics, or poetic expressions such as *Moonsheered* shown with an art deco typeface and star symbols. Cindy Fletcher-Holden describes a boat's name as the icing on the cake. "Whether a boat is bought new or used, there are always issues to deal with. It might be the engine, refrigeration, or fresh water, or perhaps the mast didn't come in time, or the sails weren't cut right—the list goes on and on. But when it comes time for the boat name, it is the cheapest part of the process and the most fun part for the new owner."

Megayachts tend to have the most traditional boat names and designs of all, and the production of the name is often handled by someone other than the owner. If the owner wants something simple and classic, tradition dictates gold-leaf roman or italic type with a dark outline around the letters. Carla Christopher, of BoatArt.com in Fort Lauderdale, Florida, says that when customers ask for a traditional or elegant design, "They are thinking of Times Roman lettering."

Basing the design of your boat's name on the boat's length is one approach, though probably not the best one. A better starting point, once you've determined the name, is to consider whether the name lends itself to a purely typographic solution or could be enhanced by an integrated image—and whether you have enough transom space to comfortably position a more complex graphic. A type-only design is by no means a compromise or lesser solution; in many cases it is just the right choice. Conversely, too much imagery can create visual overload.

In the corporate world nearly every product or service has a brand. A brand has many facets, one of them being visual. In a full branding effort, a company's logo is one key component used in the larger effort to communicate the culture of the company to customers. In any random sampling of logos, some (called *logotypes*) are purely typographic, some (called *symbols*) are image-driven, and some (called *logomarks*) use a combination of type and image. Each of these categories includes some of the most widely recognized corporate logos.

A well-chosen typeface coupled with a smaller, well-integrated illustration can create visual interest without adding whimsy.

Moonsheered

Flyin' Low

REMEDY

WANDERIN' ★ STAR ★

Coca-Cola is a logotype, Prudential is a logomark that includes a distinctive typeface and "the rock" symbol, and Nike has achieved ultimate brand recognition with its "swoosh" symbol, which is so ubiquitous that the logotype rarely accompanies the symbol anymore. Each of these logos is highly recognizable, and none is rendered clearly superior to the others by the inclusion of more or less type or imagery. A similar approach to branding can apply to your boat's name because in essence you are creating a personal logo.

Elizabeth   *Windswept*

Commercial Script was designed by Morris Fuller Benton in 1906.

Elizabeth   *Windswept*

Park Avenue was designed by Robert E. Smith in 1933.

Elizabeth   *Windswept*

Zapfino was designed by Hermann Zapf and David Siegel in 1998.

The use of 30-point type for each example above makes it easy to see how differently each script is drawn. Comparing x-heights (the height of a letterform as measured from the baseline to the top of a lowercase "x") reveals the variation in size between Park Avenue and Zapfino. Those differences can suggest why one style may better fit your boat's name than another. If you were Elizabeth, which would suit you?

Typography Only

A type-only design is traditional for boat names, but a modern typeface in a well-designed composition can make your boat name seem perfectly contemporary. A type-only name doesn't have to feel predictable or historical.

Traditional

If your boat's design and name are both classic, following tradition makes sense. To develop a classic name, select a typeface with historic roots. Serif typefaces such as Bembo, Caslon, Garamond, Goudy, Bodoni, Baskerville, Jenson, Palatino, Sabon, or Times New Roman all derive from fifteenth- to nineteenth-century European sources. A truly classic design uses serif capital letters for the boat's name and smaller sans serif capitals for the hailing port. No further embellishments are required.

Script lettering is also classic in appearance. Scripts are calligraphic, more like handwriting than serifs and sans serifs. They can be formal or informal and vary dramatically, just as handwriting does. If you choose a historic female name or a name that seems best expressed by using flowing, often-connected letterforms, consider a script. Formal scripts such as Snell Roundhand, Shelley, Commercial, and Edwardian all have connecting lowercase letters (often with small x-heights), swashes for some of the uppercase letters, and an oblique stress (forward slant) to the letterforms. Styles such as these are commonly used on engraved invitations and stationery to connote a proper, elegant, or dignified affair. Formal scripts work best as a combination of initial capital letters followed by lowercase letters. Scripts should *not* be used for successive capital letters. And because scripts have a smaller x-height, they may need to be set at a larger size and with a little extra tracking (spaces between letters) to improve legibility.

Commercial Script, Park Avenue, and Zapfino are more stylized formal scripts. Commercial Script is traditional, Park Avenue has a retro feel, and Zapfino is lyrical and can be dramatic. Names such as *Elizabeth* or *Windswept* communicate different feelings when set in each of these types.

Liquidity

Charisma

EASTPORT

SPLENDOUR

SISSY HANKSHAW

A sampling of script (*Liquidity, Charisma*), display (*Punch Buggy, Splendour*), and slab serif (*Sissy Hankshaw*) styles.

And there are opportunities for creative enhancement of a classic design. Such stylistic additions as arched baselines, outlined letters, dropshadows, swash initial letters, delicate underlines, and simple scrollwork can add sophisticated detail without overpowering a name.

Contemporary

The majority of boat names are contemporary and feature contemporary designs. There are thousands of typefaces to choose from and endless ways to compose the letterforms. There are informal scripts, slab serifs, sans serifs, and display faces. Informal scripts such as Mistral and Rapier appear active and quick, while Brush and Athletic scripts imitate the brushstrokes of a sign painter, and Tekton, Suburban, Marker, Freestyle, Fabulous, and Bullet scripts are all appropriately named to suggest something about their appearance.

Slab serifs—including Rockwell, Triplex, ITC American Typewriter, Memphis, ITC Officina Serif, and Aachen—express names in a solid, weightier style. Originating in England in the early nineteenth century, slab serifs were used in combination with dropshadows and outlining to add more drama to advertisements and broadsides. Commonly seen on sports- and collegiate wear today, slab serifs are often set in all capital letters.

Sans serifs are more contemporary in nature, most being designed in the twentieth century. Consider Franklin Gothic, Futura, Frutiger, Gill Sans, Helvetica, Trade Gothic, or Univers. The style differences that distinguish one sans serif from others include whether its round letters, such as "o," are geometrically or organically shaped. Compare the lowercase "a" in Futura with that in Gill Sans. Futura is considered a geometric sans serif because its letterforms are based on circles, lines, and right angles and its stroke weights are uniform, while Gill Sans is known as a humanist sans serif because its forms come closer to calligraphy.

Display faces are the most common fonts on the menus of sign companies and boat graphics suppliers. Each display typeface is stylized to convey a culture, geography, emotional state, personality trait, period in history, or something completely experimental. Some are plainly expressive and others are highly ornamental. The name of the typeface often suggests its appearance: Broadway looks art deco, Get Jiggy is in motion, Old English uses German blackletter forms, Rickshaw has an Asian flair, Critters is made up of small animals, Giddyup references lasso shapes, and Scratch looks itchy. Recognizing the intent of

Boat Name

Futura was designed by Paul Renner in 1925.

Boat Name

Gill Sans was designed by Eric Gill in 1927.

the typeface is important for clear communication. A typeface such as Lithos, which is modeled after Greek stonecutting, would send a confusing message if used to display a contemporary pop culture name. Display faces offer a predictable way to ensure that your typographic choice pairs well with your boat's name, but they may not be the most inventive approach to name design.

Designing with Type

In a type-only solution, the choice of typeface is the single most important decision. Researching options on the Internet is easy and recommended. Many websites that sell typefaces (either the original foundry that developed the typeface or a distributor that sells many type designers' work) offer previewers in which you can type in the name of your boat and select a typeface to view it in. This allows you to sample various styles for appropriateness and appeal. The websites of boat graphics providers likewise have font menus, although their choices can be more limited. (A list of these resources can be found on page 163.) Professional boat letterers have extensive font libraries on hand and can help you select the right typeface. You can also draw your own lettering to be digitized, though this option is best left to those with skilled hands.

Once a typeface has been selected, there are other typographic and compositional considerations. Options such as shadows, outlines, arching, and gradations are all available, but a good designer will also look for other typographic nuances within the name. Could some letters be bigger or smaller, could some nest within each other, or would there be added visual interest if a name with multiple words occupied more than one line? Might all lowercase letters work better than all capital letters, or should there be a mix? Would an irregular baseline enhance the concept? In the name *Windswept,* for example, an oversize swash capital "W" could be followed by lowercase italic letters with progressively more space between them. The color of the letters could also become subtly lighter, the result being a name that appears to be sweeping away. Or the letters "w" and "e" embedded in the name might present an opportunity to emphasize the first-person plural of boat ownership "we" if that is meaningful to those aboard.

Looking again to corporate logotypes as examples, many have typefaces designed specifically for them or are carefully crafted with

Windswept

Cochin Italic was designed by Matthew Carter in 1977.

windswept

Set in Filosofia Regular designed by Zuzana Licko in 1996.

Archer

Chicago C

Kedzie KEDZ

Darwycke

Squirt Blizza

French Script

Tekton, TEKTO

Brush, BRUSH

Script Bold

SNYDER SP

Calligrapher

Broach. BRO

Caxton, CA

GOUDY, G

Avant Garde

F

TIMES   ABCDEFGHIJKLMNOPQ
abcdefghijklmnopqrstuvwx

GARTH   ABCDEFGHIJKLMNO
acdefghijklmnopqrst

CHARTER   ABCDEFGHIJKLMNO
abcdefghijklmnopqr

FLASH   ABCDEFGHIJKLMNOPQRS
abcdefghijklmnopqrstuv

BROADWAY   ABCDEFGHIJKLMNO
abcdefghijklmnopo

MARKER   ABCDEFGHIJKLMNOPQRS
abcdefghijklmnopqrst

RICKSHAW   ABCDEFGHIJKLMNOPO
abcdefgijklmnopqrstu

Athletic   ABCDEFGHIJKLMI
abcdefghijklmnopqrstuv

Brush   ABCDEFGHIJKLMNOF
abcdefghijklmnopqrstuvw

Mistral   ABCDEF

FL 1234 FA

BLOCK

TIMES

CASUAL

STACCATO

AMERICANA

JESTER

BENNY

BOOKMAN

De VINNE

PAPYRUS

ENTINE

TORIAN

an off-the-shelf typeface in which individual letterforms have been manipulated to communicate a desired concept. The manipulation can be subtle—a perfect example of this being the logotype for FedEx. The typeface is a sturdy sans serif in which all of the letterforms have been positioned to carefully touch so that the capital "E" and lowercase "x" form a white, right-facing arrow in the negative space between the two letters. The other letterforms have also been manipulated to give the logo crisp and pleasing negative and positive spaces. And the two contrasting colors, purple and orange, used to accentuate the compound name are effectively bright and bold. All these choices add up to a logotype that connotes a solid, strong, forward-moving company without relying on gimmicks or excessive ornamentation. The uniqueness is in the intervention.

WINDSWEPT in Bembo

WINDSWEPT in Times

It may be that an unmodified typeface is all that is needed for your boat's name. Using *Windswept* as an example again, the name could be beautifully presented by choosing the typeface Bembo, which has a "crossed-stem" capital "W" as part of its design. Since there are two "W's" in Windswept, choosing Bembo over Times New Roman will give the name a more distinctive appearance. The crisscrossing "W's" conceptually and visually suggest crosswinds. Seeing what the letters of a name look like in various typefaces can be a helpful way of choosing a font. Or it may be that swapping a letter from one typeface for another allows a name to come alive. The key is to think about what your name means conceptually, then look for opportunities to communicate that idea visually.

Typography as Image

There are highly stylized typefaces made from drawings of bones, rope, animals, snow-capped mountains, or any number of other items. Choosing one of these can be a quick solution for a boat name. Why not put *Y KNOT* in a typeface made of rope or show *Hot Coles* in type that appears aflame? These are simple examples of using typography to create images—although predictable and easily replicated by other boatowners. Other, more complex ways to morph type into image include manipulating or positioning words to create dimension, space, or new images.

The results can be unique and effective if done well. Common downfalls include pairing a name and its expected typeface, such as *Y KNOT* in the rope typeface, when so many other interesting solutions are possible, and forcing mismatched letters and words together. Both are tempting design solutions that produce disappointing results. Highly stylized typefaces that are an exact visual representation of the name can be seen as tongue-in-cheek design solutions (see the discussion of kitsch below) or simply as clichés. They are the equivalent of a one-line joke. If your intention is an over-the-top design, approach it in a way that shows you really mean it.

Forced typographic solutions are even harder and often yield designs that are awkward and unattractive. A popular example of forced type is letters stretched into the shape of a fish, fins and all. Though this approach might be conceptually appropriate for the name in question, few names will conform easily to a fish shape without illegible letter distortions. One way to make the design more successful is to situate the name within the large area of the fish's body and draw the other needed parts of the fish in a style that is compatible with the type.

Gumball shows that letters can form fish shapes, but it is a challenge to make it work. The gradated background helps to make the letters read together while adding some dimension to the illustration.

Well-designed boat names using typography as image take time to develop. They are not for the faint of heart or the need-it-today boatowner. They are never turnkey. They require a good idea, a hefty command of typography, and the skill to render the final design effectively. But they can be highly innovative solutions when the concept is strong and the design well considered.

A potpourri of typographic styles and techniques can be used to suggest a concept with a name. The illustrative quality of the typeface itself, the substitution of an image for letters, or the highlighting of specific letters each enhances a name. *Handbasket* does fall into the visually redundant category for reiterating the name with the basket weave pattern, and *Incentive* seems an incongruous typestyle to communicate the idea of an incentive.

Using Images

It has become commonplace over the last two decades to incorporate imagery into a boat name. No boat name requires an image, but an image can make a name more visually compelling—or clarify its meaning.

Images work best when they add rather than repeat meaning. A blue whale depicted next to the name *Blue Whale* is redundant unless the whale contributes a spouting blowhole, a sassy tail flip, or some other embellishment to the design. The Internet is full of clip-art and photographic images, but that doesn't mean they're all good or visually arresting. You wouldn't hang up any old picture in your living room, so why settle for an average palm tree or an overused flying fish illustration? Existing images can be reinterpreted and custom images can be drawn. A good way to arrive at a new image may be to work with an artist or designer. While custom work can be more expensive, you can often develop an individual design at a very competitive price. If you have the talent and inclination to try your own hand, you are limited only by your imagination and the production requirements of your supplier.

When brainstorming images to accompany your boat's name, think beyond the obvious. Yes, a crescent moon would work with *Moonglow,* but could stars or another symbol from the night sky work better? If the name of your sportfishing boat demands a fish image, consider an uncommon view of a fish or perhaps a cartoon fish with features exaggerated to elaborate on the name. In *Island Hooker* the fish is seen in a frontal view that flaunts her lips.

In the days of hand painting, a letterer could illustrate any image regardless of complexity or breadth of color palette. When imagery first moved from hand to machine rendering, palettes and details were limited. Single-color flat shapes and outlines—known as line art, icons, or clip art—were all that vinyl-cutting machines could produce. Clip art uses negative and positive space with patterning to express detail and dimension. The name comes from old books of black-and-white illustrations that designers and artists could buy to "clip out" ready-made images. Often the designer or artist would manipulate the illustration in some way before using it.

Single-color vinyl cutting is still used to generate letters for boat names as well as simple clip art. Vinyl rolls are available in a fairly broad range of colors, including metallic gold and silver leaf. If a simple yellow sun shape is what you want and you're not choosy about the style of rays or other distinguishing features, it should be easy to find a ready-made clip-art sun and have it cut in yellow vinyl.

The majority of images used in boat names are still relatively simple. Clip-art images are common because they are readily available and inexpensive. Much of the artwork available at sign shops and online marine graphics websites is considered clip art. A standard library of marine motifs—fish, fishing rods, anchors, mermaids, seabirds, animals, and tropical icons—is stocked by most places. Clip-art images range from simple essences of images to colorful detail. For boat names, the drawings are generally rendered in playful, humorous, or exaggerated styles, except for sportfishing icons that aim to capture the experience of "the catch."

Digital technology has revolutionized how images can be printed on a vinyl substrate, and four-color printing—similar to that used for books, posters, and magazines—affords nearly limitless image opportunities. Anything from single colors to photographic-quality images can be rendered. Unlike a clip-art fish, a digitally rendered fish can show layers of detail like those in a photograph. Any image that can be drawn, scanned, photographed, or collaged can be turned into a digital image and printed on vinyl.

Original artwork can be created by a boatowner or by a professional artist or designer. If your concept is very specific and you have examples of what you want, there are professionals who can complete a design for you. If you would like to develop your own artwork for printing, it is imperative that you provide a high-quality image to the supplier. Guidelines are different for various types of machines, so it is best to check with your boat graphics supplier to ensure that your image is in the appropriate size, format, and resolution. (A list of resources can be found on page 163.) Alternatively, a professional can create an original design for you and handle all of the production and installation requirements.

The repetition of paw prints makes this simple clip art more interesting, although it lacks the distinctive individuality of the customized fish in *Island Hooker* or the visual complexity of the digital swordfish.

Integrating Images with Typography

It is a shame that so many boat names are displayed with familiar clip art positioned in ways unrelated to the name or concept. The possibilities are practically limitless, yet a look around almost any marina will confirm that an arching marlin centered between the first and second word of the boat name is far too common.

Your goal should be to integrate concept, typography, and imagery into a seamless design. You want a composition that functions as a single unit rather than an assemblage of unrelated items stuck onto a transom bulletin board.

Unified elements and careful placement make these strong examples of type and image integration.

Images and type can be combined in at least four ways. A large image can serve as background for the type, or an image can wrap or nestle next to a few letters in the name, or the image can be a letter accent or substitution. Finally, an image can be visually suggested from the negative spaces between letters—such as the arrow formed by the "E" and "x" in the FedEx logo. To decide which is right for your boat name, consider what each of your elements brings to the concept and composition. The next chapter includes an in-depth discussion of compositional elements and visual hierarchy that may be useful for decision-making.

A full background image necessitates a large transom and a high-quality rendering, but the result can be dynamic (see *Dragon Lady* on pages 64–65). The image and name must both remain legible, of course. The contrast between the two must be great enough that the name reads easily, yet the two elements can't compete with each other. To achieve this, select an image that provides a comfortable space for positioning the name. As in a magazine cover, you want to be able to see every bit of the image and type, and the composition must be carefully crafted to facilitate reading at every level. Pay attention to color, complexity, and contrast within the image.

The second option, placing an image near or within the type, is obvious. The key is to do it with intent and finesse. Too many designs miss the opportunity to truly integrate an image with the name and instead settle for treating them as adjacent forms. Each name offers different possibilities for integrating an image, but here are several questions to consider: Are there natural spaces in the name where an image might fit? Does the concept expressed by the name suggest where the image should be relative to the letters? Are there typo-graphic elements that might connect naturally or conceptually with elements in the image? Would adjusting the baseline or alignment of the letters provide an appropriate opening for an image? Might over-lapping or transparency offer integration? Could one or more letter-forms be altered to better frame the image? Type and image work best together when there is a deliberate connection between the two that is neither forced nor overstated.

The third technique, letter substitution, is simple and popular. You might, for example, insert a sun image or a compass rose in place of a letter "o," or substitute the handle of a fishing rod for a capital "L." A tiara instead of a dot atop the "i" in the name *Princess* is another example. Substitutions are easy to execute, don't require additional space, and can emphasize the meaning of a name by making it more explicit.

Any of these techniques can enliven your boat name. Just be sure that the concept, typeface, and image support one another without competing or being redundant. The last thing you want is an uninspired image randomly placed next to a mismatched typeface.

Sophisticated, Kitsch, Fun, Serious, or Daring?

Identifying your personal style and determining what kind of statement you want to make with your boat name will guarantee the best results. You've chosen your name for a reason, and you should be able to articulate that reason to anyone who asks. Listen to how you describe the name to someone else and remember the words you use. Your visual expression of the name should be an extension of those words. If you choose the name *Party of Four* because you and three fishing buddies have a great time in the boat four times a year, you'll want a different design from the couple who name their boat *Voyager* because they've just retired, have spent tens of thousands of dollars outfitting the boat for long-distance cruising, and plan to explore to their hearts' content. *Party of Four* wants to exude wacky fun, and *Voyager* should express the owners' serious yet adventurous nature.

Decisions come more easily once you've identified your style. You should be comfortable with what that style communicates about you to others. Brash and big, meek or mellow, your name can form a first impression and also be the final thing remembered about you long after a first introduction. All styles are viable. The one you want depends on who you are. If traditional sophistication is your thing, go after simple elegance. Similarly, if you are loud and proud, don't be afraid to show it.

Compare your typeface and imagery choices with your self-determined style to see how they fit. A contemporary sans serif type with an irregular baseline in a bright color would make sense for the *Party of Four* but would miscommunicate the meaning of *Voyager* as described here. In fashion, car, interior, or boat design we seek items that "work together," and the same should be true for boat names. Taking note of your style will also deter you from making default or generic choices that don't evoke anything in particular. There is no reason to settle for a bland design when it is just as easy to make deliberate, meaningful choices.

Once you've settled on a design, you may want to apply the same visual components to other areas of your boat or gear. You can think of the typeface and imagery you've chosen as the elements of your

Sometimes you just have to embrace the urge for kitsch. What saves this from being redundant or over the top and turns it into a successful design, is the well-drawn letters and the lyrical curve of the "L" tail.

personal logomark. If you are planning to apply your boat name to life jackets, a dinghy, baseball caps, or crew jerseys, use the design you've created. It is always a shame to see one style on the transom, another on the nameboard, and a third on cocktail napkins. You can have fun with your personal "brand" by communicating it consistently.

But don't overdo the design. As architect Mies van der Rohe famously proclaimed, "Less is more." Of course, you can subscribe to architect Robert Venturi's rebuttal, "Less is a bore," and aim for an over-the-top design, but do it well—if it fails, it will fail spectacularly. Graphic designer Milton Glaser's "Just enough is more" is, perhaps, a good middle way. Be ever mindful of how much is "just enough" to communicate your idea. Quell the desire to communicate everything.

a letterer's story

Cindy Fletcher-Holden
Fletcher Art, Annapolis, Maryland

EASY AND HARD

Cindy Fletcher-Holden is a fine artist who paints large contemporary canvases, murals, and faux finishes along with boat names. She enjoys the creativity of boat names, especially when she can have some fun with them. Mostly that fun is easy to come by, yet every once in a while something simply breaks down.

Bullfrog was a fun one. The concept was initiated by the boatowner's love of a series of Budweiser beer ads in which bullfrogs said "Budweiser" in a call-and-response style. One frog would say "Bud," and the others would respond with "Weiser." That repeated multiple times—"Bud…Weiser," "Bud…Weiser"—simulating real bullfrogs but with an unmistakable advertising message.

Focusing on the spirit of the concept, Cindy sketched a frog on the back of her work order, and the owner gave his approval on the spot. From there she took some time to compose the type, overlapping letters slightly to make a solid visual unit. Lowercase letters in a simple sans serif font give the name a casual appearance and create some visual space in which to integrate the frog.

Cindy gave the frog a goofy expression that is accentuated by his body language and the way he grasps the letters "B" and "l." Lily pads and cattails balance the name while creating an environment and a horizon. Blue and green, the natural colors for the name, also work with the boat trim.

Bullfrog is one of Cindy's favorite boat names. She had the pleasure of seeing it published in the newspaper many times because the owner was a good sailor who won many races in the boat.

Looking back at more than twenty years of painting, Cindy can remember only two occasions when things just plain went wrong. On one such occasion the job took her to a lovely home overlooking the water, with the sailboat in the water six flights of steps below. The owners offered Cindy an inflatable dinghy and suggested that she take the pump along, because the dinghy had a small air leak.

The job required painting the name on both sides of the hull and the hailing port on the transom. By the time she finished the first side, Cindy needed to pump up the dinghy. She was forced to pump again on the second side, and the dinghy was by this time feeling unstable. When she finally got to the transom, the morning had heated up, more boats were in the bay making the dingy rock, and she was still pumping and pumping to keep afloat.

Doing her best to keep going, she moved her paint cup to get comfortable for the transom work. Placing it on the deck, she prepared to pump up the dinghy one last time, but the dinghy hit the cup and sent blue paint flying everywhere. "It was at that point that I lost it!" Cindy remembers.

Her husband came to her rescue with rags, acetone, and rubbing compound, and together they scrubbed for over an hour to complete a perfect cleanup. Thoroughly frustrated by this time, Cindy still had to paint the hailing port to complete the job. Ultimately she was pleased with the results and can laugh about the fact that the boat's name was *Flying Jenny*. It was the first and hopefully only time she's spilled, and she adds that she's never yet fallen into the water—not a bad two-decade track record.

A Letterer's Story

Ray Skaines

SR Signs, League City, Texas

HOT LETTERING AND A CASE OF MISTAKEN IDENTITY

The date was December 31, 1988, and the time was almost 5:00 PM when Ray Skaines finished lettering a name for a repeat customer at the Watergate Marina. The boat was the customer's third that year. His first boat just wasn't big enough to suit him, so he had traded it in for something larger, and a few months later he upgraded again. He was Ray's kind of customer. After wishing the man "Happy New Year," Ray was on his way.

The next day Ray heard the news. Moments after his departure, the happy customer and his wife had noticed a commotion in the middle of the covered dock: A boat was on fire. The couple ran to help untie the boat and push it away, but unfortunately the fire had spread across the old covered dock's roof, and flames engulfed the entire structure. Recognizing the danger to their own boat, Ray's customers hurriedly ran back to push it, too, away from the dock—but they were too late. The bimini had already caught fire, and now the flames were threatening them. They had to jump into the water and leave the boat behind. Before that New Year's Eve was over, sixty of the sixty-three boats on Pier 7 were destroyed. Ray never lettered a fourth boat for the customer or saw the man again. He assumes the owner took his insurance money and abandoned boating forever.

Ray had an ideal working relationship with one marine dealership over the years. He enjoyed the freedom to come and go and had lettered many of their boats. On his way to a job one afternoon he stopped by the sales office to pick up the instructions. The original salesman wasn't there but a second salesman, trying to be helpful, found a note which read "sea envelope" and gave Ray that as the name. Thinking it was an unusual wordplay, but having done far stranger names using the word "sea," Ray got to work.

His design was fairly straightforward. The hand-lettering was all caps in gold with a black outline. To add interest, Ray curved the cap height line, making the letters graduate in size, and added a star between the city and hailing port. Satisfied, he was just cleaning up his brushes when the original salesman came running back to him saying "No, no, that isn't it!" Waving an envelope, he explained that his hastily written, and somewhat illegible, note said "see envelope." The true name of the boat was to be found within the envelope.

Realizing that an honest mistake had been made all the way around, Ray went back to the boat, snapped a quick picture to save as a funny memory, and started over.

SEA ENVELOPE
PEARLAND * TEXAS

Watergate Marina, Pier 7, on the
evening of December 31, 1988.

AFTER FIVE · AFTER HOURS · AFTER TAXES · AFTER WORK · ALPHA WAVE · ALTERED ATTITUDE · ANOTHER TOY · ARBITRAGE · ATTITUDE ADJUSTMENT · AWOL · AYE SEA U · BANKER BOAT · BILL COLLECTOR · BIOPSEA · BONE DOCTOR · BOSSEA · BOTTOM LINE · BOUNTY HUNTER · BRAIN DRAIN · BUDGET BENDER · BU$INE$$ · CARPETBAGGER · CASH BONUS · CHECK OUT TIME · CLEARED FOR TAKEOFF · COIN OPERATED · COMP TIME · CON-TRACT-OAR · COP OUT · DEALER SHIP · DOCKTER · DOUGH BUOY · EMOTIONAL RESCUE · EYE BALL · FAMILY THERAPY · FIELD OFFICE · FIELD TRIP · FIRE ESCAPE · FIRE POWER · FIRST FLIGHT · FIVE O'CLOCK WHISTLE · FLASH · FLY BY FREEDOM · FREELANCER · FREQUENT FLYER · FREUDIAN SLOOP · FULL COMMISSION · GOLDEN PARACHUTE · GREEN SLIP · HELLO NURSE! · HIGH FLIGHT · HOLD THE PHONE · HOME OFFICE · HYDRO THERAPY · IT'S ONLY MONET ·

work

ITSWORTHITTOO · JET LAG · JETSTREAM · JOB SITE · JUST BREATHE · KNOT ON-CALL · KNOT PRO BONO · KNOT WORKING · KRYPT KEEPER · LEGAL HOLIDAY · LIQUID ASSETS · LOAN SHARK · MEDICINAL PURPOSES · MEGA BITE · MUTUAL FUN · NAUTI NURSE · NEWS BUOY · NIGHT SHIFT · OFF CALL · OFF THE CLOCK · ON ASSIGNMENT · ON CALL · ON COMMISSION · OUT TO LAUNCH · OUT TO LUNCH · OUTLAW · OUT-PATIENT · OVERBITE · PAVING FOR IT · PETTY CASH · PLASTIC MONEY · POCKET CHANGE · POCKET YACHT · POLICY MAKER · PROFIT MARGIN · RAINMAKER · RECOMMENDED DOSAGE · RECOVERY ROOM · REELTOR · REMEDY · RISKTAKER · RIVER HOBO · SABBATICAL · SALESMAN SHIP · SALINE SOLUTION · SCENE ISLE · SEA MOVER · SEADATION · SEA-NOTE · SEAQUESTERED · STORMTROOPER · STRESS BUSTER · SUMMERS OFF · SWEET TOOTH · SYBERVESSEL · THE HEARTBEAT · THE OFFICE · THERAPY · TIME & MONEY · TOOTH FERRY · TROUBLESHOOTER · UNION MAID · WHOLESAIL · WORKING MAN · X-RAY

It's easy to guess from many names how the owner earns a living. Others such as *Keep It Up* are less obvious but can be more fun when you learn the associate meaning (a doctor treating erect dysfunction). Using an illustratio to enhance the meaning, instead of reiterating it, is a creative way to consider adding elements In *Juiceman* the apple graphic replaces the dot of the "i' and describes the type of juice.

PARTY Girl

Just Hammered

Flamingo Daze

CARPE

TEAKY

HIG

DEBAUCHERY

Blue Mar

Shaken Not Stirred

AquaHolic

HOUSTON, TEXAS

BOMBAY EXPLORE

19TH HOLE · ADRENALIN · AFTER HOURS · AMATEUR HOUR · AMORETTO · ANYTHING GOES · AWOL · BAMBOOOZLER ·

BELLY FLOP · BELLY LAUGH · BIG SHOT · BOATWISER · BOTTOMS UP · BUZZ · CHAPERON · CHEERS · CIRRHOSIS OF THE

RIVER · DOUBLE TROUBLE · DRY AND HIGH · FANTASEA · FLING · FOOTLOOSE · GOOD HUMOR · HAPPY HOURS · HAPPY

OURS · HARVEY DOCKBANGER · HELLRAISER · HIGH LIFE · HIGH TIDE · HIGH TIMES · HOCUS POCUS · INTOXICATING ·

IRISH WAKE · JAMMED UP · JOYRIDE · JUST ADD WATER · JUST FOR THE HULL OF IT · LIFE IS GOOD · LIQUID ASSET · LIVIN

LARGE · LOADED · LOCO MOTION · MISS BEHAVIN · MOOR FUN · NAUTI BOY · PAR-TEE-TIME · PIER PRESSURE · PLAY PEN ·

PURE PLEASURE · PUNCH LINE · QUICK ONE · RAY-SEA · REVELRY · RIOT TIME · RIPTIDE · RIP ROARING · ROCK & ROLL

SALOON · SIN OR SWIM · SOUTHERN COMFORT · TANKED UP · TWISTED · WET N WILD · WICKED · YACHTS OF FUN

ght Moves

Latitude Adjustment

KNIGHT - CAP

DIEM

Week's End

GREENWICH, CT

SEE SEA & 7

HOG WILD

ini

Party of FIVE

RECESS

Last Call

and play

If you are the social type with the cocktail flag always flying, you should design your boat name to reflect your party style. *Party Girl* and *Party of Five,* both designed by Carla Christopher, show an innovative use of capital and lower case letters—think of it as a party mix. Integrated graphics (including one olive for everyone in the party) and expressive type choices send a message that says welcome aboard. In contrast, the predictable script type of *Last Call* lacks energy and perhaps suggests that they've already stopped serving.

Understanding a bit about design basics may help you create, evaluate, or enhance your boat's name. As the saying goes, "a little knowledge can be dangerous," but in this case it should be helpful. Consider it as similar to the brief introduction to boating you'd give to guests who've never been on the water—it helps them get oriented, enjoy themselves, and be better crew.

Designing is an active and creative process. It's a bit messy at times. Contrary to what some believe, a good solution rarely just drops from the sky. It is usually a product of moving through a

chapter three

DEVELOPING A
DESIGN

problem-solving process that includes researching, experimenting, ideating, discussing, more

ideating, confirming, and executing—not always in neat sequence. It's always fun to get your hands

dirty, but it may take more than one try to get them clean. Whether you are creating the design

yourself or working with a letterer, the moment the name goes on your boat the process shouldn't

be evident, instead the intent should be clear and the design compelling.

A good name design melds three components: the naming concept, the elements and principles of visual design, and the use of typography.

THE CONCEPT

The concept is the source of your boat's name and the expression of what that name means to you. It may communicate something simple or complex, impersonal or deeply personal—the choice is yours. But whatever the concept may be, your design decisions should spring from and conform to it.

If your design is well executed, the concept will communicate itself clearly and convey meaning to others. If the two don't match, however, you have a tuxedo-with-sneakers scenario—it's not clear where you're headed for the evening. Even if you don't care to share the deeper meaning of your name with others, it is still "good design" to make visual choices that are consistent with the concept.

Elements

line

shape

plane

texture

value

space

color

The elements are the ingredients of a design.

Principles

unity

emphasis/focal point

scale/proportion

balance

rhythm

repetition

The principles focus on how the ingredients work together.

Composition

the overall arrangement and organization of the parts of a design

Visual Hierarchy

in a composition, what parts are seen first, second, third, et cetera

All of the elements and principles are important, but some apply to boat names more readily than others. Line, space, and color are the primary elements, and emphasis, scale, balance, and rhythm are the primary principles to consider.

Arrriba's chunky type, bright colors, and diagonal position all support the name's meaning. In *For Play,* a typical clip art image flanked by Brush Script type misses the opportunity to leverage the double entendre or play up the fun.

Thick or thin dropshadows, delicate or heavy outlines, and bright or contrasting colors all have an effect on how we "read" a name.

THE ELEMENTS AND PRINCIPLES OF DESIGN

The elements and principles of design aren't rules, but rather visual considerations that add richness to a design. They are taught in beginning design and art classes to establish a foundation, after which they can be used to critique or improve a design.

Line

The strokes used in the lettering and image can be rough or smooth, exacting or gestural, slowly or quickly drawn, and light or heavy in appearance. Lines can suggest directional movement, and they can merely suggest a visual outline or render one in great detail. The right line style helps realize the concept.

Beautifool contrasts a solid, weighty sans serif with lyrical curliques that bookend the name. The two styles elegantly suggest the two meanings of the name. And upper- and lowercase letters keep it properly informal. Also note how the slight waves in the crossbars of the "t" and "f" reference the more dramatic curiques.

Color

A full spectrum of colors is available for boat names today, so color can be used in many ways. Full color can be used to render an image with photographic detail. Color can also evoke feelings or represent a universal ideal, and color associations can vary from culture to culture. Yellow feels warm, like the sun, and in the United States, at least, red conveys warnings—think traffic lights and stop signs—and other attention-demanding messages. Choosing a single color or juxtaposing contrasting colors can also communicate in a direct way.

Emphasis

Any element of a design, or all of them together, can be used to create emphasis. Emphasis, or focal point, is the part of a design to which your eye is drawn and to which it is encouraged to keep coming back. Insufficient emphasis results in a bland design that doesn't direct your eye, but multiple points of emphasis can cause visual overload, the effect of which is not much different from a lack of emphasis. Line, color, placement, and scale are good ways to add emphasis. In a boat name, emphasis can be as simple as a beautifully arched baseline for the text or as direct as a bright red outline.

Scale

When applied to a boat name, scale means not only the sizes of individual characters, images, or accent elements, but also their collective size relative to the available compositional space (your transom).
An important consideration is deciding on size differences from one letter to the next, and between letters and any images used to add meaning to the name. Although space can be at a premium, experimenting with scale changes can enhance even the simplest design.

Balance

A sense of balance is important, but visual balance doesn't necessarily require that all objects be perfectly even or symmetrical. Asymmetry can give a sense of balance if the objects in the design are weighted appropriately. By tradition, boat names are typically centered on a transom, which is sometimes a shame—a different placement would often be more inventive or add meaning to the name's concept.

Rhythm

Normally associated with music, rhythm functions similarly in visual design. The rhythmic pulse of a boat name is typically even but can be made faster or slower. It provides a flow to the design and prevents awkward visual breaks. A name in which letters and image are not well integrated may feel choppy or lack rhythm altogether.

Composition and Visual Hierarchy

A painter has a canvas, a graphic designer has a page or screen, and a boatowner has a transom (usually) on which to compose. It is incumbent on each of these creators to use the available space to its best advantage. A boat-name design that is too big or small for its transom will look just that, and one with too many or randomly placed pieces will appear disconnected. Unlike a blank canvas or page though, transoms increasingly have more elements or equipment to take into consideration when evaluating the space and placement of the name.

Above Two examples in which erratic baselines coupled with complicated letterforms cause unsuccessful balance and rhythm.

Left *Bahama Mama* has strong flow and good integration of all elements. It is not traditionally balanced yet feels comfortable. *Yellow Jacket* uses the same illustration but changes its scale and direction for separate areas of the boat. Also note that the initial capital letters drop below the baseline of the text for added emphasis. The top image shows the hailing port treatment on the transom, and the bottom image shows the name on the boat's topside.

A good composition employs the elements and principles of design to achieve visual coherence and hierarchy. If every component floods your eye at once, the parts probably have equal visual weight, which is to say that the design lacks hierarchy. Adjusting lines, scale, or colors can change component weights to establish emphasis. This is especially true of names using letters and imagery. For example, a boat name might include a large background image of blue waves overlaid by a medium-size name in slab serif white letters, and even though the name is considerably smaller, it will gain visual weight from its strong contrast with the blue waves. Your eye would take in everything but be drawn first to the white letters of the name, which is thus the primary element in a visual hierarchy. The more components a design possesses, the more important visual hierarchy becomes. There should be a rhythm to the composition and a hierarchy that encourages your eye to land first on one part (emphasis), then easily move to other parts of the composition.

Boat-name designs that use only typography have fewer competing parts, and it is the placement and flow of those parts that make a good composition. Swash letters, initial capital letters, or other flourishes can be used advantageously to direct the eye or create an interesting or unusual balance.

And don't forget about the hailing port; it is a major visual element in the composition too. Keeping it simple is a good general rule, although it can act as a balancing element or a way to add emphasis. Choosing a sans serif typestyle and centering it below the name is standard practice, but experimenting with other options could add to your design. Incorporating it into your thinking from the beginning will give the best results; ultimately it should appear as part of the design, not an add-on.

TYPOGRAPHY

Typography imparts meaning and comprehension. Anyone who uses a computer is aware that text gets styled in a document either by default or by active choices, and most people are comfortable selecting a font, a type size, a text alignment, and line spacing. Few computer users practice what is considered "good typography" on a daily basis, however. Instead, like landlubbers tying "good enough" but inelegant knots

Logged Off has many fun elements and an interesting display typeface. Yet reducing the number of elements and varying their scale would create better visual hierarchy. The design is also complicated by the position of the boat manufacturer's logo, which, because of its similar size and position, can be seen as part of the design. *Big Play* demonstrates that well integrated type and graphics establish visual hierarchy and flow.

(remember, if you can't tie good knots, tie lots of them!), we forge ahead, and though the result may lack all typographic nuance, it's done and it's functional. Yet a few small changes can take your boat's name up a typographic notch. Trained letterers have a depth of typographic knowledge, but some sign shops and online sources may not.

"quotation marks" "prime marks"

Here a close quote (for the end of a quotation) is used where an open quote (beginning a quotation) would have been more appropriate. An open quote looks like two inverted commas.

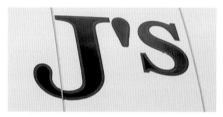

This prime mark should be replaced with a single close quote.

Letterspacing straight from the software isn't always ideal. Too much space, as in *Egg,* makes a word difficult to read, especially if it is many characters long. Too little space, as in *Wish,* causes legibility issues from lack of character separation. And poor spacing between an initial capital letter and the following lowercase letter, seen in *Sea,* is common. *Friends* would be better spaced if a ligature was created with the "R" and "I" to move them closer together. These typographic challenges are ideally corrected within the software prior to outputting the vinyl letters, but adjustments are possible during the application as well.

Here are five rules that can improve anyone's typography—
on or off the water:

1. **Know the differences among punctuation symbols and marks.**
   Quotation marks and apostrophes should be curly, or *smart*, while inch
   and foot marks, also called prime or hatch marks, should be straight
   up and down, or *dumb*. Quote marks should be used sparingly in all
   venues ("air quotes" should be outlawed altogether) and don't really
   have a place in a boat name.

   There are three mid-height horizontal lines—the humble hyphen
   and two types of dashes. The hyphen is shortest and is used to connect
   pieces of a word or compound words, as in "mid-height." An en dash
   is slightly longer and is used to connect a range, as in "the 1969–70
   around-the-world sailboat race," a phrase stitched together with one
   en dash and two hyphens. The em dash is the longest of the three and
   delineates a break in thought in a sentence—as here, or as in the first
   sentence of this paragraph. If you use any of these in your boat's name,
   don't add a space on either side. Some manual spacing might be necessary, but a full space is not proper typesetting.

   Note that some display-style typefaces lack a full complement of
   punctuation marks and symbols. A substitute may be offered, or
   nothing at all may be available. If you need a symbol you can't get
   from the typeface you've chosen, you'll need to try another typeface.

2. **Adjust the spacing between letters to prevent large gaps or letters that
   are too close.**
   The goal is not to make every space mathematically equal, but to
   give the visual *appearance* of even spacing. Minor manipulations
   can increase the legibility of your boat's name. If a typeface is well
   designed, the space between two letters (known as *kerning*) should
   not need much adjusting, but even a well-designed typeface sometimes leaves too large a space between an initial capital letter and the
   following lowercase letter, especially if the capital letter is larger or
   ornamental. As *MotorBoating's Guide to Boat Maintenance* said way
   back in 1955, "Remember, a well-spaced plain letter is better than a
   poorly executed fancy letter." An easy way to tell if the spacing looks
   good is to squint your eyes.

3. **Don't distort a typeface by artificially extending, condensing, bolding, or italicizing it.**
Doing so ruins the integrity of the letterforms. Instead, choose a typeface designed with the qualities you seek. With so many typefaces to choose from, it should be easy to find one that communicates what you want. Tempting distortion buttons may be available in your software or online, but they do a poor job of manipulating letterforms.

4. **Limit the amount of emphasis.**
Or said another way, if everything is emphasized, nothing is emphasized. Combining bold letters, bright colors, an outline, a dropshadow, an underline, and quotation marks would result in visual overload. Select just a few techniques to put emphasis where it is needed.

5. **Don't make type too big.**
Consider how big the type really needs to be. Using the tools of composition and visual hierarchy, determine the appropriate size by evaluating your space and the components of the design. The general tendency is to err on the big side—to fill the space. Leaving some *white space* (blank space) is usually desirable, as you see on this page.

Attention to these five conventions should be easy, with the exception of correcting letterspacing. Some software programs don't let you adjust spacing problems manually. In particular, online preview software may not accurately render letterspacing or allow you to adjust it. In such instances you can make the necessary spacing adjustments as you adhere the letters to your boat's transom.

Artificially condensed

Artificially extended

The typeface Scala has been manipulated. Notice how narrow and awkward the "y" looks in the condensed version and how drawn out the "f" is in the extended version.

These names strike the right balance of emphasis. *Benbow* uses several elements—including bold decorative type, outlines, and a thick drop-shadow—and *Free Life* mixes point sizes, upper- and lowercase letters, decorative letters, and a curved baseline. The overall effect in each is compelling, not overwhelming. *Dragon* keeps things simple by allowing its highly illustrative typestyle to communicate the name's meaning.

BUZZ OFF

A Word on Coast Guard Regulations

Boating laws since 1918 have been repealed and amended many times, including major over-hauls in 1940, 1958, 1971, and 1983. As of 2006, all documented vessels in the United States are required to display a name and hailing port on the hull, and commercial boats are further required to display the name on each side of the bow. Undocumented boats need not display a name or hailing port, but those with propulsion machinery are required to register with their state of primary use and to display the registration number prominently on the hull.

Recreational boats under five net tons cannot be documented, while those over five net tons may be documented at the owner's discretion. Certain advantages derive from documenting, but that's not the subject of this book—nor is a definition of net tonnage, which has more to do with interior volume than weight. Suffice it to say here that the great majority of recreational boats are undocumented and therefore need not display their names and hailing ports. Though not required to do so, however, the majority of boats over 16 feet choose to display a name and port on their stern.

United States Coast Guard rules for naming documented boats require that the name be no longer than thirty-three characters, that it not be identical to words that could be used to call for help, and that it not be obscene or profane. Given how common some names are, the hailing port is an important secondary identifier. The name and hailing port must appear together, in characters at least four inches tall.

Most of the Coast Guard guidelines are adhered to voluntarily by undocumented boats, except that making the characters of the hailing port four inches high creates a visual hierarchy problem. Since the characters of the hailing port are smaller than those of the boat name, the latter would have to be considerably taller than four inches to comply. The result on most boats would be a graphic too large for the transom. Letterers generally use their best judgment to scale the components appropriately for legibility and the size of the boat.

www.uscgboating.org/safety/fedreqa/reg_numbers.htm

Buzz Off makes a statement with its direct no-nonsense style—and may even be a wordplay if Buzz is truly off—but it might create some confusion in an emergency VHF radio call.

WORKING WITH A PROFESSIONAL LETTERER

Prior to vinyl lettering and web-based technology, a boatowner almost always hired the services of a letterer or sign shop to paint the boat's name, so every name was a custom job. Few owners considered a do-it-yourself paint job regardless of their boat's size. Even if the name was simple and the design straightforward, someone with hand skills did the lettering.

Today many customization opportunities are available, and there is every reason for boatowners to consider their options. The key to a well-designed boat name is to know your aspirations and recognize your limitations. If the design process isn't something you want to tangle with personally, or if you enjoy creative collaboration and know your limitations, hire a professional.

To get the most out of the experience, consider these few notions in advance:

If your boat's name or its meaning is unusual, give the letterer any background information you have. This will help him or her generate ideas and will save time, which in this instance is money. Letterers are interested in the story of your boat's name, though they may not be as interested in the story of your life!

Despite the seemingly limitless possibilities for boat names, yours may not be as original as you believe. This is no problem at all—you selected the name for a reason, and the reason is no less valid if the name is not unique. It just means that your letterer may have worked with that name before and can guide you to a design solution that is unique to you. Articulating what the name means to you will help the letterer make the appropriate distinctions.

Identify your particular design biases or physical restrictions (such as limited transom space) in advance so you can share them with the letterer. Don't be afraid to say that you hate blue or that the color must match the blue of your hull striping. If there is a particular feeling you want to evoke or message you want to communicate, make that clear.

Who are the decision-makers for the design? If you and your boat mates hold veto power, make sure you share your ideas or concerns with the letterer at the outset so that false starts are avoided.

To avoid surprises and set expectations for everyone including yourself, make known up front how much involvement you choose to have in the design. The common scenarios follow.

Giving the Letterer Free Reign

If you have selected a boat name but have no preconceived ideas about the design, give the letterer free reign to develop concepts for you. (This assumes, of course, that you've seen samples of the letterer's work and like the quality.) Expect to receive two or three initial designs, and understand that the letterer should be compensated for his or her time. Initial designs aren't a free estimate; they are usable design solutions. Ask about charges ahead of time.

Seeing the initial design solutions will be fun, and some of them may surprise you—in a good way—with their inventiveness. Once you've reviewed them, be honest and forthright in your response. If you love an idea and are ready to go, do it! If your preferred solution is close to one of the concepts, describe the elements you like and try to isolate the part that needs revising. If nothing appeals to you, be constructive and clear in your comments, identifying things you like and don't like in the existing designs. Thinking about the elements and principles of design will help you organize and frame your critique.

Letterers typically build one round of revisions into their price. Generally a second round of design solutions is all that is needed to arrive at your design. After you've decided, the letterer will ask you to sign off on the design and will put the job into production.

Collaborating with the Letterer

Most boatowners have ideas but not a clear picture in their head. Professionals are receptive to these ideas and use them to inform their creative process. You can show the letterer a sketch you've done by hand or on the computer; you can show samples of logos, brands, typefaces, images, boat names, or other design pieces you like (perhaps using this book!); or you can look through the letterer's portfolio of boat names and point out elements that appeal to you. The goal is to provide a sense of your interests and preferences while leaving room to experiment. In this scenario you understand that the letterer will add his or her expertise to the design process, and the end solution may drift from your starting point.

If you want a specific component incorporated into the design, make that clear. The letterer should respect your request and develop ideas based around it. If he or she has concerns about your idea—such as its quality or its resonance to the concept—he has a duty to tell you.

As in the free-reign scenario, the letterer will present initial design solutions for your approval or feedback. When the design phase is complete, the letterer will ask you to sign off on the design and will put the job into production.

DESIGNING IT YOURSELF

Designing a name yourself can be an outlet for creative expression and a source of pride every time you see it. Use what you've learned about design basics to evaluate and refine your work. Once you are ready to execute the design, you'll find it beneficial to contact a letterer or sign shop. Something that looks ideal on your computer screen may not have the proper resolution or quality for reproduction, and the earlier you know this the better your results. Show the letterer or sign shop your design so they can confirm the correct preparation of type and imagery, and if you are open to suggestions, you might be pleased with any tweaks they suggest. They might offer a nuance that hadn't occurred to you. After you've finished installing the boat name, sit back and enjoy your work.

All kinds of stories can be conveyed through the design of your name. *Zoom's* crew is caricatured individually, while in *Lady T-Rex* the dinosaurs represent the boat-owner as a mother whose children are always running from her. *Thisismyboat* is a cheeky play on the notion of a name yet a definitive statement of who is onboard.

Thisismyboat.

A Letterer's Story

H. A. "Bud" Gillespie
Retired Boat Letterer, Wichita, Kansas

THE CROWNING ACHIEVEMENT

Like many sign painters of his era, Bud Gillespie learned his craft at the Philadelphia Technical Institute under the GI Bill after serving in the navy in World War II. Early in his career, Bud owned the Media Sign Company in Media, Pennsylvania, where his work was recognized by *Signs of the Times.* His truck graphics for an office supply company, a Best of the Month winner in 1957, showed his humorous and inventive style. A filing cabinet shoots out file cards that hold the company's name, while the image of a typewriter anchors the text on the truck door. Bud built a successful business painting signs of all types and enjoyed working with a variety of materials and constructions.

In the 1960s Bud moved to Florida with his wife and four children. There he began a thirty-plus-year career hand lettering boats, sometimes two or three per day, building a pleasurable and lucrative livelihood. Some ninety percent of the jobs were conventionally painted in imitation gold letters with an outline to match the boat's trim color, but he found ample opportunities to do creative names.

Sadly, most of the images of his work were lost when his portfolio was destroyed in a fire. One of the remaining images, *Dragon Too,* shows Bud

with his granddaughter Taylor in 1993. He was close to retirement then and still hand painting, never having made the move to vinyl letters. *Dragon Too* used letterforms with angular elements that referenced Asian brushstrokes. Bud painted a meaningful ligature of the "R" and "A," with the tail of the "R" pointing down to an upward-pointing dragon's tail that is topped with an arrowhead.

Bud's long, productive lettering career has given him great satisfaction and many crazy stories (he admits he likes to have fun), but he says his crowning achievement in the art of boat lettering was not a special boat name design but a portable floating platform that allowed him to easily letter boats anywhere. Lightweight for transporting and simple to tie to a customer's transom, it was also flexibly designed to adjust to all styles of sterns. With it Bud could get close enough to work while having eight feet of lengthwise space on which to maneuver. Bud conceived of this platform after years of uncomfortable and impossible lettering situations, and he constructed variations to accommodate on-land lettering and lettering on small sterns. He is still surprised that none of his competitors ever copied his invention.

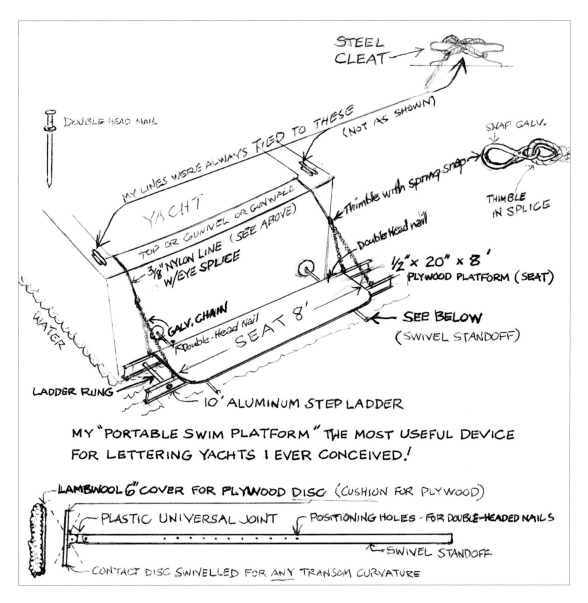

STEEL CLEAT

DOUBLE HEAD NAIL

MY LINES WERE ALWAYS TIED TO THESE (NOT AS SHOWN)

SNAP GALV.

Thimble with spring snap

THIMBLE IN SPLICE

YACHT

TOP OR GUNNEL OR GUNWALE

3/8" NYLON LINE (SEE ABOVE) W/EYE SPLICE

Double Head nail

1/2" × 20" × 8' PLYWOOD PLATFORM (SEAT)

GALV. CHAIN

Double-Head Nail

SEAT 8'

SEE BELOW (SWIVEL STANDOFF)

WATER

LADDER RUNG

10' ALUMINUM STEP LADDER

MY "PORTABLE SWIM PLATFORM" THE MOST USEFUL DEVICE FOR LETTERING YACHTS I EVER CONCEIVED!

LAMBSWOOL 6" COVER FOR PLYWOOD DISC (CUSHION FOR PLYWOOD)

PLASTIC UNIVERSAL JOINT — POSITIONING HOLES - FOR DOUBLE-HEADED NAILS

SWIVEL STANDOFF

CONTACT DISC SWIVELLED FOR ANY TRANSOM CURVATURE

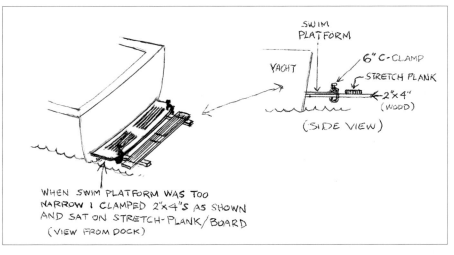

SWIM PLATFORM

YACHT

6" C-CLAMP

STRETCH PLANK

2"×4" (WOOD)

(SIDE VIEW)

WHEN SWIM PLATFORM WAS TOO NARROW I CLAMPED 2"×4"S AS SHOWN AND SAT ON STRETCH-PLANK/BOARD (VIEW FROM DOCK)

GRANDE FINALE

PALOS PARK, IL

TIME

Leisure

Linger Longer

Endless OCEANSIDE,

No Mo Sno

OLD-TIME
COS COB, C

Noah Genda

Liv Inn

Silver Lining

got time

Sea renity now!

Our Time Out

Halcyon Day

Script typestyles are popular with full-timers. *Got Time* takes advantage of a contemporary script and all lowercase letters to express a casual, fun look. *Grande Finale* is a great example of blending tradition and smart design. Its style harks back to hotel names of the early 20th century, and its elements are classic (serif capital letters and gold-leaf letters). The well-considered typographic composition features stacked words, enlarged "bookend" letters, a curved baseline, and scrollwork to create an elegant, cohesive design with plenty of visual interest.

retired

ABLE TOO · ABOUT TIME · ADIEU · AMBLE ON · BEEN THERE · BIG MOMENT · BITTER END · BLUE YONDER · BY CHOICE · CATHARSIS · CUTTIN LOOSE · DAILY DOUBLE · DILLY DALLY · DRIFTWOOD · DOUBLE DIAMOND · DUO · EACH OTHER · EVER US · EZ GOIN · FELLOWSHIP · FINAL CALL · FINE FETTLE · FLORIDAYS · FOREVERMORE · GO FOR IT · GOLD COAST · GOLDEN HOUR · GOLDEN JUBILEE · GOOD FORTUNE · GOOD LIFE · GOOD 2 GO · GRANDSTYLE · HAPPY OURS · HARMONY · HEYDAY · HOME · IDLE OURS · IDYLL · IT'S ABOUT TIME · JETSET · JOINT EFFORT · KEEL OVER · KEEPSAKE · LAST CHANCE · LAST HURRAH · LATE BLOOMER · LAZY DAYS · LEGACY · LIBERATED · LIVIN END · LOAFERS · LOFIN · LONGEVITY · LONG WAIT · MAGIC TOUCH · MIGHTY GREAT · MONEY TO BURN · MY TIME · MY TURN · NEVERMIND · NEW LIFE · NOT A CARE · OLD FRIEND · OLD HAT · OLD SALT · PARTING SHOT · PINNACLE · PIPE DREAM · PRIME TIME · REMINISCE · RICH UNCLE · ROAMER · ROYAL FLUSH · SAIL AWAY · SECOND WIND · SPARE TIME · STILL GOING · SUN QUEST · SUN SEEKER · TIMELESS · TIME OUT · TWILIGHT · UP AND AWEIGH · VAMOOSE · WANDERLUST · WHILE AWAY

racy

Sexual innuendo and descriptions of relationships can offer greater visual expression, although most boat-name designs err on the side of decorum. Suggestive illustrations such as in *Huntress* or in *Rug Burn*, (the female graphic reminiscent of those seen on a trucker's mud flaps) are outside of the norm. However, their typestyles and graphics support the names' meaning by adding to the story, not reiterating it.

ADONIS • ADULTERER • AFFAIR • AFLAME • AFTERGLOW • AFTERNOON DELIGHT • AGLO • AGONY AND ECSTASY • AH SIN •

AMOROUS • AYE SEA U • BACHELOR • BARE BOTTOM • BE MY GIRL • BERTH CONTROL • BEST LOVE • BEWITCHING •

BLOW JOB • BORN LOVER • BOSSA NOVA • CALL GIRL • CATCH U • CHARMER • CHEAP THRILLS • CLIMAX • COCKEYED •

COED • CORK SCREW • DALLIANCE • DARLING • DOUBLE TROUBLE • ECSTA SEA • EGG-STA-SEA • ELOPE • ENRAPTURE •

ESCAPADE • FANTASEA • FETCHING • FLAME • FLIRT • FONDLE • FOOTSIE • FRENCH KISS • FRISKY • FROLIC • GETTIN' BUSY •

GIGOLO • GYRATION • HANDS ON • HEART THROB • HOT LIPS • HOW WAS IT FOR U? • HUSTLER • JEZEBEL • JOINT VENTURE •

LIL DARLING • LOOKER • LOVE NEST • MAKE OUT • MESS AROUND • MI BUDDY • MISS BEHAVIN • NAUGHTY • OGLE •

PHILANDERER • PINCH ME • PLAY BOY • PLAY THING • PURE PLEASURE • QUICKIE • RAUNCHY • RAY SEA • RENDEZVOUS •

RISQUE • ROMP • SASSY • SAY MAYBE • SCREAMER • SCREW LOOSE • SEA COWBOY • SEADUCER • SEADUCTION • SINFUL •

SPRING FLING • SWAGGER • TAKES TWO • THE MISTRESS • TICKLER • TRYST • TWO'S COMPANY • TYME TO PLAY • UNZIPPED •

VIRILE • WAGES OF SIN • WE DID IT • WET AND WILD • WET DREAM • WICKED

Prior to the advent of vinyl lettering, a paintbrush and paint,

a steady hand, and a good eye were the tools needed to letter

a boat. A letterer's toolbox typically contained paints, an

assortment of squirrel-hair brushes, a mahl stick (see below),

masking tape, grease pencils, linseed oil, and turpentine.

Maintenance was easy too. Brushes were stored in baby oil

to preserve the suppleness of the bristle hairs, and everything

else was simply wiped free of excess paint and placed back

in the box.

Today a boat name can be painted, made from vinyl, carved

in a nameboard, or cut as three-dimensional illuminated

letters. A boatowner can have the name designed in whole or

in part by a professional or do the entire job himself. Brick-

and-mortar sign shops (often chains) are on the street, and

marine graphics virtual storefronts are open online twenty-

four hours a day.

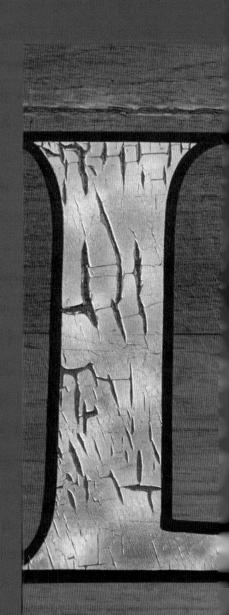

Vinyl letters and graphics are easily the most prevalent medium for boat names today, for many reasons. Vinyl is durable, economical, widely available, and easy to apply and remove. But that is not to say that other techniques shouldn't be considered. Each offers something different, and depending on your boat and personal style, one of them might hold the ideal solution for you.

HAND PAINTING

To appreciate the ease with which a boat name is now designed, printed, and applied, you have only to hear the experiences of early boat letterers. If you've been humbled attempting to apply your own vinyl name, you will appreciate how much greater were the challenges of the pre-vinyl days. For decades, articles in boating magazines that offered how-to advice on hand painting would preface their explanations of the process with phrases such as "practice, patience, rapt concentration" and "an art few people master" as a warning to novices. Seasoned letterers tell of painting names from a floating dinghy or, more harrowing yet, while hanging upside down over the transom. If you have trouble just writing your signature these days, imagine painting it perfectly while bobbing upside down.

Artists and letterers who still hand paint are not as easy to find as they used to be; there are fewer and fewer with the necessary skills. When hand painting was the primary technique, professional letterers either freehanded or used a pounce pattern to create the name. When freehanding, the letterer would tape or snap a baseline and cap height for the lettering, mark a middle point on the line as a reference, then work back on either side of the middle to sketch in the letterforms with grease pencil or crayon. Letterers also used these guidelines to ensure a crisp edge on the letters by painting onto the taped line and then pulling off the tape when finished. Some seasoned letterers considered guides a crutch, believing that if you understood the letterforms and had a steady hand, only paint and brush were needed.

The first step in the production of *Dragon Lady* was to use a pounce pattern to create a faint outline of the drawing on the transom. See page 65 for the finished transom.

The pounce pattern technique began with a paper print of the boat name that had been typeset to the desired specifications. A pounce wheel, a small metal-toothed wheel similar to a sewing tracing wheel or a pizza cutter, was then run along the edges of the typeset letterforms to perforate the paper with small holes, creating a dotted stencil. The stencil was then positioned and taped on the boat's transom, and the letterer would gently hit a pounce stick—a stick with a powder-filled pillow on the end—against the stencil to leave a light, dotted tracing of the boat's name on the transom. After removing the stencil, he or she would then paint in the name, cleaning off any remaining powder at the end of the job.

The craft of hand lettering is notable for its nuanced creativity. An understanding of letterforms, proportions, typestyles, and design affords a letterer unlimited opportunities to break free from standard conventions to paint ligatures, swashes, comingled characters, and whatever else might enhance the meaning of a name through the design of its letterforms. Outlines, dropshadows, highlights, flourishes, and underlines might be incorporated with the letters, as well as symbols, icons, or other graphic devices. The integration of these elements in the final graphic gives the letterer artistic freedom of expression. For instance, dropping the tail of a capital "R" below the baseline and wrapping the "O" next to it might suggest romance in one name, while adding a dimensional shadow might add more strength to another. These gestures, intuitive to the letterer, give a name more meaning and presence. Regional letterers are recognized for their unique styles or known for their fluency in combining letters and artwork.

To form the vertical parts of letters, the painter uses up-and-down brushstrokes with the tip of the brush held high. The brush is flattened for the curves, which are always painted from the inside of the letter, working out to the edges. The mahl stick, a crucial tool for some letterers, is held in the opposite hand with its cushioned tip leaning against the boat. A mahl stick is a wooden dowel with one rounded, fabric-covered end. Its function is to provide a supported place on which to rest the painting hand to steady the brushstrokes. Letterers who don't use a mahl stick often use their opposite forearm to steady the working hand. Jokingly nicknamed a "whiskey stick" by older letterers, it was also known to calm the shakes.

When it's time to apply the paint, One-Shot, a sign painter's enamel, is poured into a small plastic cup and taped to the side of the boat so

Left With the outline of the artwork visible, another stencil was used to add the letters.

Above Carla Christopher adds more detail to the painting while hanging upside down.

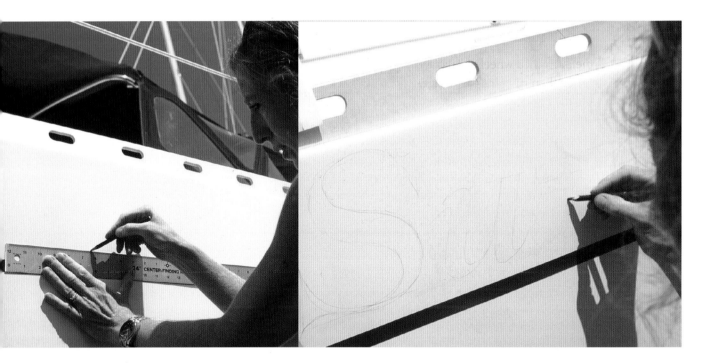

Cindy Fletcher-Holden
painting *Suzee*.

that the paint will be nearby yet both hands can be free. The letterer must work quickly and with sure strokes to guarantee a smooth, even, high-gloss finish with the quick-drying paint. The enamel is called One-Shot for many reasons, one being that you have only one shot at laying it down well. The preferred choice for its smooth application and easy mixability, One-Shot enamel is less toxic than it used to be, having been reformulated without lead.

Because hand painting is the original method for crafting a name, it is seen as traditional, authentic, and often "old-school." Though desired by owners of classic wooden boats for precisely that reason, hand painting has broader applications. Skilled letterers and artists can paint inventive names in a full palette of colors and styles—and a proper application of paint and varnish can last as long as vinyl with little maintenance.

GOLD AND SILVER LEAFING

A boat name rendered in gold or silver metallic vinyl with a dark outline is timeless and common, particularly on large yachts. Gold or silver leafing done by hand is less common, however, because the skills required aren't practiced as much, and there is a marked difference in appearance between the two.

Vinyl stock has expanded to offer solid metallic colors and other pre-made patterns of gold and silver that imitate hand leafing, such as Florentine Swirl and Engine Turn. Such patterns are available at two price points, the less expensive of which only resembles gold leaf, while the more expensive actually contains a gold admixture, usually 22 karat. As you would expect, the latter has a more realistic appearance. Silver metallic is used less often because historically it hasn't been as stable as gold, although silver vinyl suffers fewer oxidizing problems than silver leaf.

These crabbing boats proudly retain their hand-painted names on their nameboards. They are in contrast to the more decorative hand-turned gold leaf names below.

The engine-turned gold-leaf styles—which are characterized by a pattern of touching circles—highlight the greatest difference between pre-made vinyl and hand leafing. The vinyl version, readily available in two sizes of circles, is perfectly consistent in circle size, pattern, spacing, and finish because it is machine generated. In contrast, hand turning creates a regular but not perfect pattern with a true gold finish and a burnished patina. The overall result of hand leafing is pleasing because the circles have more character and the burnished finish undulates. More important, the circle size can be custom proportioned to fit the letters. In vinyl, the pattern can look too big or small depending on the letter size.

To make an engine-turned pattern by hand, the letterer begins as for gold leaf without a pattern. Once a paper-thin layer of real gold leaf is adhered inside the letterform outline, however, a wadded soft cloth, often velvet, is pressed and rotated against the gold layer, imprinting one circular movement at a time. The circle shape is then repeated in a horizontal pattern, row after row, until the inside of each letter is patterned. The letter outline is painted once any excess leaf has been removed, then the whole name gets a coat of varnish to secure it.

Labor-intensive and customized, engine-turned gold leaf was used for commercial signage in the early- to mid-twentieth century and is still seen on the lettering of some fire trucks and ambulances—where it hasn't been replaced by vinyl. The businesses and services (law firms, accountants, doctors) that used engine-turned gold-leaf signage were a reflection of the prestige associated with the style. In the late 1950s, boating publications such as *MotorBoating* offered how-to guides for gold leafing boat names—not only demonstrating its popularity but acknowledging its difficulty. There are still traditionalists, romantics, and craftspeople who agree that sometimes technology is no match for the beauty of handwork—and this is especially true when a full teak transom is in need of a name.

Valhalla not only features hand engine-turned gold leaf but is also a rarely seen example of painted dimensional shadowing. It is lettered on a 1934 Playmate Series wooden motoryacht that is a sister ship to Ernest Hemingway's *Pilar*.

EFGHIJKLMN

Balance pride v

Howard Rogers of The Raven Maritime Studio in Annapolis, Maryland, is one of the few carvers who still earns a living at his craft. His shop is filled with an overwhelming array of beautifully carved letters, nameboards, and signs. One sign shows each step of the carving process, highlighting the precise, labor-intensive effort involved. The photographs above show examples of the unique lettering styles Howard has developed over the years. A visit to Howard's shop is a lovely glimpse of a handcraft that may eventually be lost as fewer boatowners request nameboards and fewer artists know how to hand carve.

CARVED NAMEBOARDS

Traditionally nameboards were made by wood-carvers who hand chiseled a boat's name into a plank, usually teak or mahogany, after which they would finish the letters in gold leaf or paint. Skilled carvers could faithfully delineate the serifs, stroke weights, and counterspaces of individual typestyles, but they also developed their own custom alphabets. Their thorough understanding of how best to form letters through carving yielded special typographic treatments and techniques.

One practical advantage of a nameboard is that it can be removed and reused with little effort or damage. Currently nameboards find a place on boats with little transom space or in conjunction with other naming devices. As with hand painting, sometimes they are preferred by yacht owners simply for their traditional appeal. The aesthetic component varies for better or worse with the ability of the maker. Most boards now are carved in sign shops with a router, which follows the shape of digitally generated text and is only as good as the typography it follows. If a typeface lacks good kerning or proper punctuation, or the designer setting the digital typography doesn't follow accepted typographic conventions, the result can be a poorly crafted name. The precision of a router does afford sharper serifs, more even stroke weights, and greater consistency than can routinely be achieved in handwork. While a clean finish is the signature of the router, special effects such as simulated hand carving are available. They can't, however, replicate the best hand-carved lettering with its evident attention to kerning, ligatures, and nuances of individual letters.

Calliope's vinyl letters are adhered to a wooden board. *C d' Amore* and *Bobcat* are traditional nameboards with gold-leaf letters—although somewhat unusual for their use of lowercase letters.

VINYL BOAT GRAPHICS

Vinyl boat names are ubiquitous for good reason. Vinyl is affordable, easy to use, flexible to design with, and readily available. The ascendance of vinyl was breathtakingly swift. Prior to the mid-1980s, vinyl lettering was available only as individual self-adhesive letters, and the job of aligning and neatly spacing a full name was of interest only to the most devoted DIYers. In 1983, however, *Yachting* magazine's "Gadgets and Gilhickies" section featured an article on applying a vinyl name as a single sheet, and single-sheet vinyl was standard by the mid-1990s.

The revolutionary shift from hand painting to vinyl technology turned on the development of a single machine. This innovative piece of technology, called the Gerber Signmaker III, was an automated lettering system introduced by Gerber Scientific Products in 1983. It enabled letterers and sign makers to output type as cut vinyl letters. A simple machine, the Gerber Signmaker III is comparable to the

Above A vintage Gerber Signmaker IVB, Graphix 4, originally offered in 1985.

Right Typefaces such as Brush Script, used for *Baby Beluga,* were hallmarks of early vinyl lettering. Note the poor letterspacing after the "B" 's.

Baby Beluga

computerized label makers available today at any office supply store, but it was called the Signmaker III because it could do three things: cut vinyl, pounce patterns, and make pen plots. It produced a continuous line of cut vinyl letters up to twelve inches high and could hold a limited number of fonts, each of which came on its own disc that had to be bought separately. The most common fonts included Helvetica Bold, University Roman, Optima Bold, Clarendon Bold, and Brush Script.

At first letterers and sign shops had to balance the cost of the equipment against the quality and speed with which they could hand letter. The letter-cutting time of the early equipment was so slow that hand lettering was often more efficient and cost-effective. Creativity was another point in favor of hand lettering, since the vinyl technology was limited to a narrow range of letter sizes, typestyles, and colors.

In particular, because the fonts were very expensive, few shops had an extensive library. As a result the same typestyles appeared on boat after boat. Each shop was sure to have at least one serif and one sans serif and a few scripts, but often not much more. Outlines, shadows, or any other effect required a second run of the cut vinyl letters and could be tricky to apply, so many letterers opted to hand paint such effects in the early years. Another limitation was that the rolls of vinyl for letters came in a limited palette, meaning that the same typestyles in the same colors were commonplace through the late 1980s. What the early years of vinyl offered in efficiency was offset by a lack of creative options.

Although initially many letterers believed that their creative freedoms and even their livelihoods were challenged, most embraced the technology. Constant innovations wooed the skeptics, and by the mid-1990s anyone doing boat names without vinyl was considered a "signosaurus" in the trade. After a steep learning curve and a considerable financial commitment, letterers found that working digitally could be as inventive and effi cient as painting. Letterers had access to innova tive drawing programs, enormous font libraries, and the ability to develop multiple ideas quickly. Some techniques that had been difficult to do well in paint, such as blends or gradations, became simple. Options for including imagery, adding dimensionality, or exploring nearly limit less color variations opened up new design pos sibilities. Because of these sweeping changes, the term "boat lettering" is now interchangeable with "boat graphics."

For boatowners, the benefits of a vinyl name are undeniable. Two of the most touted features are durability and ease of removal. Vinyl manufacturers provide a guarantee of three to ten years, depending on the vinyl grade, and for the most part a vinyl name can be easily removed by either peeling the edge with a sharp fingernail or, for a more stubborn application, heating the vinyl with a hair dryer to loosen it for peeling. Another

Today vinyl is available in an array of colors and metallic finishes.

Break Time

MARATHON, FLORIDA KEYS

Archa

handy feature is that if a letter gets damaged, it can be repaired by nearly any sign shop, and if damaged beyond repair it can be reordered from the original supplier. The key to making quick changes or cleanups is to have on file the specifications of your boat's name (typestyle, color, and size) along with a photograph so that a correct match can be made.

Easy on, easy off, and easy to order, vinyl boat names are available from local sign shops, national chains, boat show booths, or online. The options range from simple four-inch black letters to complex and colorful graphics that are priced accordingly. Vinyl technology supports nearly any concept and design, and as with any new technology, the possibilities expand with time. If you are looking for a custom or semi-custom design, it is best to work with a professional who has experience designing boat graphics. Any sign shop can output vinyl letters and graphics, but not all understand the specific needs of your name on your boat. A letterer can make your boat name come alive.

Nearly any design is possible in vinyl. The key is to make choices that match your name to your intent.

Vinyl Boat Graphics Websites

Boat graphics websites offer the opportunity to design your own boat name. If you have do-it-yourself inclinations or buy and sell boats often, or want a straightforward, economical solution, there are many web storefronts that specialize in vinyl boat names and other marine accessories.

Marine graphics websites provide lists of naming suggestions, font choices, and effects along with a palette of colors from which a design can be developed. The web interface offers an interactive step-by-step process and has a preview function to allow you to experiment with many options before making a decision. Depending on the boat graphics storefront, the range of possible design elements can be quite large. Once you've settled on a design, the vinyl graphics are shipped to you ready to be adhered. This system appeals to the creative side of some owners and to the efficiency instincts of others who know exactly what they want and just need a place to order.

Building a boat name this way can be fast and fun. The made-to-order approach focuses on combining existing elements from a given set of choices. This narrows what can be overwhelming possibilities to a manageable number. On the other hand, it does mean that another boat, by making the same selections, can sport the same graphics. Considerable customization is possible without the danger of a twin, but it isn't the way to craft a unique design.

Disadvantages of the web interface are a lack of flexibility to adjust individual letterforms and no ability to integrate artwork directly with the lettering. Among the available text effects are arc shapes, shadows, or distortions (artificially slanted, condensed, or extended letters), but the choices for aligning artwork within text include only right, middle, left, or underneath. Staggered lines of text or unusual alignments can't be built into the design.

Missing also is a good method for ensuring that graphics will be properly sized or proportioned. The web interface suggests measuring the total width of available area for the graphics and then offers to distort them as necessary to fit your space. Depending on the length of the name and hailing port, this can result in an unexpected size relationship among elements. It also doesn't take into consideration any other features of your boat's transom that may need to be incorporated or worked around.

The final complication is that some web interfaces can't preview the name, hailing port, and any images together. Each element is selected separately, so it's hard to envision whether the size relationships (hierarchy) will work or what the entire ensemble will look like. The good news is that when the graphics arrive, the name will typically be separate from any images, so you do have the flexibility to configure the composition any way you wish.

All such obstacles can be overcome. The key to working online is to take advantage of the considerable opportunities and understand the limitations. Boat graphics websites have the capability to do customized artwork. They offer levels of individualization if you include specialized directions or want to work directly with someone on the vendor's staff. You can also incorporate your own images by sending them to the vendor. Virtual storefronts aren't all faceless entities; many also have a brick-and-mortar counterpart.

Eagle *Eagol*

In each design of *Eagle* the boat's owner has selected an available chancery-style typeface. While an appropriate choice for a bird considered regal, it may be too common a way to distinguish each boat's name.

Knot Again

Knot Normal

Knot Bad

Y-Knott

Y Knot?

Halcyon Daze

Halcyon

DESTINY   Destiny

HUNTRESS   HUNTRESS

Names and style choices sometimes go together. *Knot* runs the gamut of kitsch possibilities, whereas *Halcyon* calls for a script typeface. *Destiny* varies depending, perhaps, on how an owner views his or her destiny, and *Huntress* is still shown in the all capital letters that are traditional for a female name.

DIMENSIONAL SIGNAGE

The newest twist in boat names involves the largest yachts and some of the more custom sign shops found on the web. What these web companies advertise is not a do-it-yourself order form but an invitation to consult with designers about illuminated three-dimensional lettering. These boat graphics come closer to commercial signage in appearance than they do to boat lettering, and because of their cost and installation requirements are applicable only to big boats. The qualities that make illuminated boat names appealing, such as nighttime visibility, dramatic color and lighting, and greater dimensionality, have parallels that go back to the introduction of neon and electric signage.

A high-tech advancement from earlier dimensional names made from screw-on plastic letters, these illuminated names are often installed on the bridge superstructure instead of the transom. Just as commercial boats and passenger ferries used nameboards because the construction of their sterns didn't offer space for a name, mega-yacht sterns are being designed for functional or recreational benefits that preclude space for the name. Sometimes illuminated signage on the topsides of the boat is coordinated with smaller vinyl graphics on the transom.

Three-dimensional signage may be edging ahead of vinyl letters in experimentation. Possibilities for dramatic colored lighting effects can enhance even a simply designed name. Changes in scale and alignments for the lettering and images are often highly innovative, and formal design decisions frequently seem to evoke the boat's name effectively. Custom typefaces are pushing new limits too. Names are more text- than image-driven, so typographic quality and ingenuity are critical. Some names have a true commercial logo quality though, which may not appeal to every boatowner.

Illuminated signage can be more than ten times as expensive as vinyl technology, so the incentive may be greater to design something unique. Each job is more custom than vinyl, too, involving fabrication, electrical wiring, and finishing processes as well as an out-of-the-water installation that is much more invasive. It is worth the time to do research and get recommendations for a quality supplier. There are a limited number of companies that specialize in these signs so you'll want to find one that not only offers the best design ideas but is also committed to good service.

There is an exciting array of surface materials, layering options, and finishes, along with monochrome and inter-changable color lighting choices. The differences between day and nightime viewing should be considered when making all decisions.

Options for cutouts, colors, imagery, and positioning make each dimensional yacht sign custom work. Erring on the side of simplicity reduces the danger of your boat's name looking like commercial store signage.

A Letterer's Story

Renee Anderson

Signs by Renee, Marathon, Florida

SWEET AND SCARY

In one of Renee Anderson's favorite naming stories, she had a happy audience for her work. The boat was on a trailer in the yard of the owners, a retired couple. Upon Renee's arrival they set up a small table between two lounge chairs and brought out a pitcher of iced tea. As Renee worked they sipped their tea, talked, laughed, and enjoyed watching her.

Eventually the wife asked Renee if she knew why their boat was named *The Mildew*. Before Renee could answer, the woman said that her name was Millie and her husband's name was Dewey. And if that wasn't reason enough, she said, the battle they waged against the mildew on their boat should be. The couple laughed, and laughed some more. They were so sweet that Renee just wanted to hug them.

Renee remembers another customer who was a lot less huggable. The man called at 5 AM asking her to come right away to letter his boat. When she suggested that he wait until her shop opened at 8 o'clock, he was adamant that she come immediately. After hurriedly preparing her supplies, she arrived at the marina in the predawn darkness. Working under lights set up for her by her customer's shifty-looking crew, she removed the boat's existing name and painted the new one (this was in the pre-vinyl days).

Unbeknown to Renee, she had been hired by drug smugglers who had just come in from a pickup and wanted to head out again with the new name. "That was when smuggling was really popular in Florida," she says. "When the boat got busted with pot, I realized who—or what—my customer had

"80" PROOF
CHOKOLOSKEE, FLA.

JOE RIMKUS JR. / Miami Herald Staff

ederal agents and police officers scour fishing boat during drug sweep in hokoloskee.

"80" PROOF
CHOKOLOSKEE, FLA.

"80" Proof and *McRich* were two other boats lettered by Renee in the 1980s whose owners were busted for trafficking drugs. In the photo above, *McRich* is shown loaded with pot.

been." After receiving a call from the district attorney, she worried that she might somehow be implicated.

Eventually she was called to testify. When asked if she'd changed the name, Renee said yes. "People don't just change names on boats," the prosecuting attorney said, but Renee replied, "Yes they do; they change them all the time. People buy a boat and I paint them a name. That's what I do."

Because Renee wasn't involved, she was eventually able to laugh about it. But she will never accept another job at 5 AM.

ADRIFT · ASTRAY · BACKDRAFT · BAKED WIND · BARELY A WAKE ·

BAY SPRAY · BETWEEN THE SHEETS · BIONIC WIND · BLADEWAKE ·

BLOWER · BLOWING IN THE WIND · BLOWZY · BLUE SKIES · BREAK

FAST · BREAKWIND · BREEZE · BREEZY · CAPTIVE WIND · CHOPPY ·

CIRRUS · CLEARSKIES · CLOUD NINE · CROSSWIND · DEAD CALM ·

DEEP-C · DEVIL'S WIND · DOWN WIND · DRIFT WOOD · ECLIPSE · EVEN

TIDE · FAIR WIND · FINGERLING · FOG CUTTER · FOR SAIL · FRESH

BREEZE · GONE WITH THE WIND · HARD TACK · IRISH WAKE · KITTI

WAKE · LUNA MAR · MAKIN MEMORIES · MARINER · MERRY WEATHER ·

MOON JELLY · MOONCHASER · MOONDANCER · MOONGLOW · MOON

WAKE · MOVIN STAR · MY LITTLE WATER LOG · NATURE CALLS · NEW

MOON · NIGHT · NORDWIND · QUIET STORM · RAINY DAY · RED SKY ·

RIP TIDE · RIVER DANCER · RIVER MIST · ROLLING THUNDER · SAND

BLAST · SEACLIPSE · SECOND WIND · SEVEN SEAS · SIROCCO ·

SQUALL · STARDUST · STILL WATERS · SUMMER BREEZE · TACKY

**wind
and water**

of Tides

NIGHTWIND

Seabreeze

WAVE

Child

Crimson Tide

SUMMER WIND
GREENWICH, CT.

Salty

Mist

WindSong

WAVELENGTH

acapella wind

The forward motion of winds or tides corresponds to the forward-leaning qualities of script type and italics. From the quirky swash "R" in *Summer Wind* to the straight-forward bold sans serif italics in *Seabreeze* to the curvilinear base-line and interconnected lines in *Night Wind,* each name reflects a sense of fluidity and motion.

Whether in jest or in earnest,
some of the most illustrated boat
names refer to fishing experiences.
Graphics of fishing rods and swordfish abound to the point where the
same images are often overused.

fish'n fun

AFISHIANDO · A FISHIN SEA · A FISH TOO FAR · ANGELFISH · ANGLER · ARTIFISHAL · B4 REEL · BAITED

BREATH · BEERACUDA · BILL COLLECTOR · BLUES BUSTER · CAPTAIN HOOK · CATCH 22 · CATCHY · CAUGHT ·

CHASER · CHUMMER · CODFATHER · COD SQUAD · CRABBY · CRAPPIE · CRAWDADDY · CRITTERS · DATE BAIT ·

DEBAITABLE · DORSAL FIN · DREAM BAIT · DRY FLY · EASY MARK · EEL-VIL · ENDORFIN · FAIR GAME · FIGHTING

FISH · FISH STORY · FISH TALES · FISH TANK · FISHCAPADES · FISHFULL THINKING · FISHIN IMPOSSIBLE ·

FLYING FISH · FOR REEL · GO DEEP · GO FISH · GOLDFISH · GONE FISSION · GOTAWAY · HAIRY CLAM · HARPOON

HOOKED · HOOKED · HOOK LINE AND SINKER · HOTROD · ISLAND LURE · IT'S CATCHING · LITTLE HOOKER ·

MINNOW · NIGHTLY CAPER · NUCLEAR FISHIN · OCTOPUSSY · OFF THE HOOK · PAN FRY · PERCH · PIRANHA ·

POLLIWOG · RAW SEA · REEL DEAL · REEL ESTATE · REELIN GOOD · REEL LADY · REELTIME · ROD BENDER ·

ENDNOTES

Chapter One

PAGE 9
Ramses II Who Propitiates the Aton...
Lionel Casson, *Ships and Seamanship in the Ancient World* (Baltimore, Maryland: Johns Hopkins University Press, 1995), 348–49.

None of these names...
Dilwyn Jones, *Boats* (Austin, Texas: University of Texas Press, 1995), 66–68; Dilwyn Jones, *A Glossary of Ancient Egyptian Nautical Titles and Terms* (London: Kegan Paul International, 1988), 8–12.

Single word attributes...
Lionel Casson, *Ships and Seamanship in the Ancient World* (Baltimore, Maryland: Johns Hopkins University Press, 1995), 351–53.

PAGE 10
The origin of the practice...
Peter D. Jeans, *Seafaring Lore & Legend: A Miscellany of Maritime Myth, Superstition, Fable, and Fact* (Camden, Maine: International Marine/McGraw-Hill, 2004), 4, 310.

Roman ship names included...
Lionel Casson, *Ships and Seamanship in the Ancient World* (Baltimore, Maryland: Johns Hopkins University Press, 1995), 351–53.

Ancient vessels were adorned...
Lionel Casson, *Ships and Seamanship in the Ancient World* (Baltimore, Maryland: Johns Hopkins University Press, 1995), 344–46.

Name devices...
J. S. Morrison, *Greek and Roman Oared Warships* (Oxford: Oxbow Monograph, 1996), 209.

PAGE 13
An ancient wall drawing...
William Murray, "A trireme named Isis: the sgraffito from Nymphaion," *International Journal of Nautical Archaeology* (2001): 30.2, 252–53.

PAGE 19
Names also included descriptors...
Ian Friel, *The Good Ship* (Baltimore, Maryland: Johns Hopkins University Press, 1995), 38.

Names also included descriptors...
George Neilson, "Ships Names, 1300–1500," *Notes and Queries* (1894): 8th S.VI. Dec. 8, 442.

From the mid-1400s...
Ian Friel, *The Good Ship* (Baltimore, Maryland: Johns Hopkins University Press, 1995), 83, 154.

Compound names...
J. K. Laughton, "Names of Ships," *Notes and Queries* (1892): 8th S.II. Nov. 26, 426.

One of the most ornate ships...
Ian Friel, *Maritime History of Britain and Ireland c. 400–2001* (London: The British Museum Press, 2003), 149.

PAGE 21
His drawings...
Irene De Groot and Robert Vorstman, *Sailing Ships* (New York: The Viking Press, 1980), ills. 26, plate 192.

PAGE 22
The inscription reads...
Irene De Groot and Robert Vorstman, *Sailing Ships* (New York: The Viking Press, 1980), 56.

England's Navigation Act...
Act 7 and 8 Wm.III.cap.22, AD 1699.

An act of Parliament...
Act 26 Geo.III.cap.60, AD 1786.

PAGE 26
Cornelius Vanderbilt...
Ross MacTaggart, *Golden Century: Classic Motor Yachts, 1830–1930* (New York: W. W. Norton & Company, 2000), 11, 15.

PAGE 27
Steamships of the late 1800s...
Erik Hofman, *The Steam Yachts: An Era of Elegance* (Tuckahoe, New York: John de Graff, 1970), 27–28.

PAGE 28
According to one...
Harper's Bazaar, 1874, vol.7 issue 21, 334.

A 1910 article...
MotorBoating, July, 2004, 136.

PAGE 31
Trade statistics show...
Yachting, 1957, vol. 101.1.

PAGE 36
Driven by a good economy...
The Boating Industry, *"1985 Estimates of the Size
of the Recreational Boating Industry,"* The Boating
Industry, 1985.

PAGE 40
For example, in 2006...
Kiri Blakeley, "Bigger Than Yours," *Forbes,*
March 27, 2006: 160.

PAGE 41
If you have difficulty...
Mark Bechtel and Stephen Cannella, "Go Figure,"
Sports Illustrated (2005): vol. 102, issue 13.

In 2004 Boating World...
Megan Kearns, "Currents: Survey Says," *Boating
World* (2004): vol. 25, issue 10, 18.

PAGE 42
As the story goes...
Stephen Johnson, www.gilligansisle.com/
minnow, 2/20/08

Chapter Two
PAGE 54
To one letterer...
Helm Wotzkow, *The Art of Hand-Lettering, Its
Mastery & Practice.* 1st ed (New York: Watson-
Guptill Publications, 1952), 32–33, 257.

Pages from lettering books...
Charles Wagner, *Blue Print Text Book of Sign and
Show Card Lettering,* 1926; Helm Wotzkow, *The
Art of Hand-Lettering, Its Mastery & Practice,* 1952;
Ross F. George, *Speedball Textbook for Pen &
Brush Lettering,* 1960.

PAGE 62
The first Hot Wheels...
Randy Leffingwell, www.powells.com, 10/11/06.

Commonly available to any resident...
Jeff Minard, ALPCA, from e-mail 5/31/07.

PAGE 63
According to Daniel Spurr...
Daniel Spurr, *Heart of Glass: Fiberglass Boats
and The Men Who Built Them* (Camden, Maine:
International Marine, 1994), 180.

PAGE 64
The 1980s constituted a watershed...
The Boating Industry, *"1985 Estimates of the Size
of the Recreational Boating Industry,"* The Boating
Industry, 1985.

PAGE 68
Although argued by some type historians...
Robert Bringhurst, *The Elements of Typographic
Style. 2nd ed.* (Vancouver: Hartley & Marks
Publishers, 1999), 97.

PAGE 77
There are thousands of typefaces...
All of the typefaces named within this book are
available for purchase; please see page 163 for
resources.

The manipulation can be subtle...
The FedEx logo was designed by Landor
Associates in 1994.

Chapter Three
PAGE 103
Design Principles and Elements...
David A. Lauer and Stephen Pentak, *Design
Basics.* (New York: Wadsworth Publishing,
2007).

Chapter Four
PAGE 140
This innovative piece of technology...
Gerber Scientific Products, www.gspinc.com,
6/19/05.

BIBLIOGRAPHY

Nautical

Artof, Susan D. *Boat Naming Made Simple. 3rd ed.* Thousand Oaks, California: The Center Press, 1999.

Bassett-Lowke, W. J., and George Holland. *Ships and Men.* London: George G. Harrap and Company, Ltd., 1946.

Bradford, Gershom. *The Mariner's Dictionary.* New York: Weathervane Books, 1952.

Casson, Lionel. *The Ancient Mariners.* Princeton: Princeton University Press, 1991.

———. *Ships and Seafaring in Ancient Times.* Austin, Texas: University of Texas Press, 1994.

———. *Ships and Seamanship in the Ancient World.* Baltimore, Maryland: Johns Hopkins University Press, 1995.

Chapman, Charles F. *Piloting, Seamanship and Small Boat Handling.* New York: Motor Boating, 1953–54.

Corcoran, John, and Lew Hackler. *Let's Name It.* Camden, Maine: Seven Seas Press, 1987.

De Groot, Irene, and Robert Vorstman. *Sailing Ships.* New York: The Viking Press, 1980.

Finamore, Daniel. *Capturing Poseidon: Photographic Encounters with the Sea.* Boston: Peabody Essex Museum, 1999.

Friel, Ian. *The Good Ship.* Baltimore, Maryland: Johns Hopkins University Press, 1995.

———. *Maritime History of Britain and Ireland c.400–2001.* London: The British Museum Press, 2003.

Grassby, Richard B. *Ship, Sea & Sky: The Marine Art of James Edward Buttersworth.* New York: Rizzoli, 1994.

Herreshoff, L. Francis. *An L. Francis Herreshoff Reader.* Camden, Maine: International Marine, 1978.

Hofman, Erik. *The Steam Yachts: An Era of Elegance.* Tuckahoe, New York: John de Graff, 1970.

Jeans, Peter D. *Seafaring Lore & Legend: A Miscellany of Maritime Myth, Superstition, Fable, and Fact.* Camden, Maine: International Marine/ McGraw-Hill, 2004.

Johnstone, Paul. *The Sea-Craft of Prehistory.* Cambridge: Harvard University Press, 1980.

Jones, Dilwyn. *Boats.* Austin, Texas: University of Texas Press, 1995.

———. *A Glossary of Ancient Egyptian Nautical Titles and Terms.* London: Kegan Paul International, 1988.

Lane, Carl D. *American Paddle Steamboats.* New York: Coward-McCann, 1943.

Lloyd's Register of American Yachts. Lloyds Register of Shipping, 1903–88.

MacTaggart, Ross. *Golden Century: Classic Motor Yachts, 1830–1930.* New York: W. W. Norton & Company, 2000.

Morrison, J. S. *Greek and Roman Oared Warships.* Oxford: Oxbow Monograph, 1996.

National Maritime Museum. *Van de Velde Drawings. Volume 1.* London: Cambridge University Press, 1973.

Newell, Gordon. *Ocean Liners of the 20th Century.* New York: Bonanza Books, 1963.

Plowden, David. *End of an Era: The Last of the Great Lakes Steamboats.* New York: W. W. Norton & Company, 1992.

Robinson, Bill. *Legendary Yachts*. New York: MacMillian, 1971.

Rosenfeld, Stanley. *A Century under Sail*. Reading, Massachusetts: Addison-Wesley Publishing Company, 1984.

Spectre, Peter H., and David Larkin. *Wooden Ship*. London: Cassell Illustrated, 1995.

Spurr, Daniel. *Heart of Glass: Fiberglass Boats and The Men Who Built Them*. Camden, Maine: International Marine, 1994.

Stammers, Michael. *Figureheads and Ship Carvings*. Annapolis, Maryland: Naval Institute Press, 2005.

Time-Life. *Time-Life Seafarers Series, Ancient Mariners*. New York: Time-Life, 1980.

Torr, Cecil. *Ancient Ships*. London: Cambridge University Press, 1894.

Zimmerman, Gene T. *Bronze Age Ships*. Pensacola, Florida: Louis Davison, 1970.

Design, Lettering, and Typography

Bringhurst, Robert. *The Elements of Typographic Style. 2nd ed*. Vancouver: Hartley & Marks Publishers, 1999.

Cabarga, Leslie. *Logo, Font and Lettering Bible*. Cinncinati, Ohio: HOW Design Books, 2004.

Cavanaugh, J. Albert. *Lettering and Alphabets*. New York: Dover Publications, 1955.

Dwiggins, W. A. *Layout in Advertising. Revised ed*. New York: Harper and Brothers, 1948.

Goudy, Frederic W. *The Alphabet and Elements of Lettering*. New York: Dorset Press, 1989.

Hanna, Jay S. *Marine Carving Handbook*. Camden, Maine: International Marine, 1976.

Heller, Steven. *The Education of a Typographer*. New York: Allworth Press, 2004.

Heller, Steven, and Louise Fili. *Typology: Type Design from the Victorian Era to the Digital Age*. San Francisco: Chronicle Books, 1999.

Heller, Steven, and Mirko Ilic. *Handwritten: Expressive Lettering in the Digital Age*. New York: Thames and Hudson, 2004.

Lauer, David A., and Stephen Pentak. *Design Basics*. New York: Wadsworth Publishing, 2007.

Longyear, William. *Type Specimens for Layout, Printing, Lettering*. New York: Watson-Guptill Publications, 1940.

Lupton, Ellen. *Thinking with Type*. New York: Princeton Architectural Press, 2004.

Margolin, Victor. *The Politics of the Artificial: Essays on Design and Design Studies*. Chicago: University of Chicago Press, 2002.

Meggs, Philip. *A History of Graphic Design. 3rd ed*. New York: John Wiley, 1998.

Morison, Stanley. *American Copybooks*. Philadelphia: William. F. Fell Co. Printers, 1951.

Nesbitt, Alexander. *The History and Technique of Lettering*. New York: Dover Publications, 1998.

Norman, Donald. *The Design of Everyday Things*. New York: Basic Books, 2002.

Petrucci, Armando. *Public Lettering, Script, Power, and Culture*. Chicago: University of Chicago Press, 1993.

Wagner, Charles L. H. *Blue Print Text Book of Sign and Show Card Lettering*. Boston: Wagner School of Sign Arts, 1926.

————. *The Story of Signs*. Boston: Arthur MacGibbon, 1954.

Wong, Wucius. *Principles of Form and Design.* New York: John Wiley, 1993.

Wotzkow, Helm. *The Art of Hand-Lettering, Its Mastery & Practice. 1st ed.* New York: Watson-Guptill Publications, 1952.

Related

Csikszentmihalyi, Mihaly, and Eugene Rochberg-Halton. *The Meaning of Things: Domestic Symbols and the Self.* Cambridge: Cambridge University Press, 1981.

Fontana, David. *The Secret Language of Symbols.* San Francisco: Chronicle Books, 1994.

Mack, Kathy. *American Neon.* New York: Universe Books, 1976.

Seymour, John. *The Forgotten Crafts.* New York: Alfred A. Knopf, 1984.

Smith, Paul. *Objects for Use: Handmade by Design.* New York: Harry N. Abrams Inc.

Museums and Collections

Independence Seaport Museum, Philadelphia, PA www.phillyseaport.org

The Library Company of Philadelphia, Philadelphia, PA www.librarycompany.org

Mariners' Museum, Newport News, VA www.mariner.org

Mystic Seaport Museum, Mystic, CT www.mysticseaport.org

Peabody Essex Museum, Salem, MA www.pem.org

Journals

American Neptune
International Journal of Maritime History
International Journal of Nautical Archaeology
INA Quarterly
Mariner's Mirror: International Journal for the Society of Nautical Research
Nautical Research Journal
Notes and Queries
Small Boat Journal

Periodicals

Boating World
Classic Boating
Cruising World
Harper's Bazaar
Harper's Magazine
Maritime Life and Traditions
MotorBoating
Rudder
SAIL
Sports Illustrated
Time
WoodenBoat
Yachting

Boat Lettering and Graphics

http://www.azinet.com/raven
The Raven Studio features an online gallery of nameboards, wood carving, and artwork of Howard Rogers.

http://www.bereng.com
Bernard Engraving offers peel and stick vinyl letters and numbers.

http://www.boatart.com
Carla Christopher offers custom vinyl boat lettering and graphics available by phone or e-mail.

http://www.boatgraphics.com
Typestries Marine Graphics offers vinyl lettering in several colors and styles, along with custom and stock graphics.

http://www.boat-lettering.com
Vinyl boat lettering and custom wooden signs. Users can send in their own graphics to add to their design.

http://www.boatlettering.net
Cap'n John's Boat Lettering features a user-friendly design and preview tool. Users can add graphics and special effects to their vinyl designs.

https://www.boatnames.net
Custom vinyl boat lettering with a design tool for name, hailing port, and registration numbers.

http://www.boatus.com/BOATGRAPHICS/names
Customizable boat lettering and graphics with a preview tool, and name application instructions. BoatUS also releases an annual list of the ten most popular boat names.

http://www.customboatnames.com
Custom vinyl boat lettering with a preview tool, along with boat-name ideas and a name generator.

http://daydream-designs.net
Lisa Hutchinson features custom boat and vehicle graphics, dimension letters, and illustrations.

http://fletcherart.net
Artist Cindy Fletcher-Holden features boat graphics, murals, illustrations, paintings.

https://www.myboatsign.com
SuperGrafix offers vinyl boat lettering and graphics with a preview tool.

https://www.namethatboat.com
Vinyl boat lettering and graphics with a preview tool.

http://www.overtons.com/lettering/custom_vinyl_lettering.shtml
Online custom lettering service provided by Overton's, a popular watersports and boating accessories store.

http://www.signsus.com/allproduct/boat_lettering_info_page.php
Boat lettering section of the SignsUS storefront, featuring an online design tool.

http://www.srsigns.com
Ray Skaines specializes in designs for signs and logos, along with vinyl lettering for boats and vehicles.

http://www.yachtsee.com
Custom vinyl boat lettering and pre-made graphics with a preview tool; also offers several lists of popular names.

http://www.yachtsign.com
Custom backlit, three-dimensional letters for boat names.

http://www.yachtsigngraphics.com
Extreme C.N.C. Yacht Signs & Designs offers custom backlit, edge-lit, and fiber-optic three-dimensional boat signs.

http://www.yachtsigns.com
Custom boat signs, hand-carved or metal, along with illuminated or non-illuminated lettering.

Typography

http://www.adobe.com/type
Easy-to-search font database from which users can purchase typefaces.

http://www.bitstream.com/fonts
Wide selection of fonts for purchase along with a directory of font resellers around the world.

http://carterandcone.com
Type foundry of Matthew Carter specializing in custom type design.

http://www.fontbureau.com
Wide selection of fonts for purchase.

http://www.fonts.com
Wide selection of fonts for purchase along with learning tools and other resources.

http://www.fontshop.com
Wide selection of fonts for purchase.

http://www.houseind.com
Wide selection of fonts for purchase, specializing in unique, contemporary collections.

http://www.itcfonts.com
Wide selection of fonts for purchase.

http://www.theletterheads.com
Group of signmakers originally formed in Denver. The Letterheads website features tips and how-to articles, along with active forums.

http://www.letterror.com
Selection of fonts for purchase along with other type resources.

http://letterville.com
Popular forum for signmakers and other letterers. The Letterville website also includes information about past and upcoming sign-making meets.

http://www.linotype.com
Large collection of fonts for purchase along with other type and design resources.

http://www.myfonts.com
Large font resource to purchase fonts and use tools such as WhatTheFont font identifier.

http://www.signcraft.com
SignCraft magazine, a popular sign industry publication, offers fonts and other software.

http://www.signdna.com/v2
Unique collection of signmakers' fonts for purchase.

http://www.stmediagroup.com
Signs of the Times, a popular sign industry publication, offers articles and examples.

http://www.typograhy.com
Type foundry of Hoefler & Frere-Jones with fonts for purchase.

http://typophile.com
Type resource featuring articles, forums, tips, and a user-created typography encyclopedia.

General Naming Information

http://www.10000boatnames.com
Large, searchable collection of boat names.

http://www.redskyatnight.com/boatnames
List of unique boat names and personal stories behind them.

http://www.uscgboating.org/safety/fedreqs/reg_numbers.htm
Details of U.S. Coast Guard regulations for the display of names and numbers on recreational vessels.

Related

http://www.1shot.com
Home of sign painters' 1 Shot paint. The website features a photo gallery, product list, and FAQ section.

http://www.archives.gov/research/guide-fed-records/groups/041.html
Archive of Bureau of Marine Inspection and Navigation records.

http://www.boat-links.com
John Kohnen's extensive collection of maritime links.

http://www.herreshoff.org/hof_02_01_yachts.asp
America's Cup Hall of Fame at the Herreshoff Marine Museum. This site features the name of every winning yacht since 1851.

http://signmuseum.org
Home of the American Sign Museum in Cincinnati, Ohio. Website features several online collections that highlight a wide range of sign types.

letterers unknown), Ray Skaines: *Nautica* (letterer/ photographer), J. Niles Clement: *Mama's Money* (photographer, letterer unknown)
Page 69: Dan Husted (photographer, letterer unknown)
Page 70: Renee Anderson: *Toy Box* (letterer) Dan Husted (photographer)
Page 71: Renee Anderson: *Toy Box* (letterer); Dan Husted (photographer, letterers unknown); Ray Skaines: *The Joker* (letterer/photographer)
Page 73: Dan Husted (photographer, letterers unknown)
Page 76: Renee Anderson: *Sissy Hankshaw* (letterer/photographer); Dan Husted (photographer, letterers unknown)
Page 79: Laurie Churchman
Page 81: Carla Christopher (letterer/photographer)
Page 82: Dan Husted (photographer, letterers unknown)
Page 83: Dan Husted (photographer, letterers unknown)
Page 85: Renee Anderson: *Island Hooker* (letterer/ photographer); Carla Christopher: *Reel Money* (letterer) Dan Husted (photographer); Dan Husted: *Cat* (photographer, letterer unknown)
Page 86: Carla Christopher: *Salty II* (letterer/ photographer); Dan Husted (photographer, letterer unknown)
Pages 88–89: Ray Skaines (letterer/photographer)
Pages 90–91: Dan Husted (photographer, letterer unknown)
Page 92: Robert Holden (photographer); Cindy Fletcher-Holden: *Bullfrog* (letterer/photographer)
Page 95: Ray Skaines: *Sea Envelope* (letterer/photographer); marina photo courtesy of Jim Flanagan
Pages 96–97: Renee Anderson: *Fowl Doc, Sea Surgeon* (letterer/photographer); Carla Christopher: *Changing Channels, Island Flyer, Keep it Up, Picante, School Bored, Slo-Flight* (letterer/photographer); Laurie Churchman: *Sea Pres II* (photographer, letterer unknown); Dan Husted: *Another Coffee Break, Big Play, Slap Shot, Jet Lag, Juiceman, Negotiator, Piano Man, Tox Docs, Yet Another Wire Nut* (photographer, letterers unknown)
Pages 98–99: Renee Anderson: *Shaken Not Stirred* (letterer/photographer); Carla Christopher: *Party Girl, Party of Five* (letterer/photographer); Laurie Churchman: *Hog Wild* (photographer, letterer unknown); Cindy Fletcher-Holden: *Recess* (letterer/ photographer); Dan Husted: *Blue Martini, Bombay Explorer, Carpe Diem, Debauchery, Flamingo Daze, Just Hammered, Knight–Cap, Last Call, Latitude Adjustment, Night Moves, See Sea & 7, Teaky Hut,*

Week's End (photographer, letterers unknown); Ray Skaines: *Aquaholic* (letterer/photographer)
Page 100: Dan Husted (photographer, letterer unknown)
Page 102: Ray Skaines (letterer/photographer)
Page 103: Laurie Churchman (photographer, letterer unknown)
Page 104: Cindy Fletcher-Holden: *Nutmeg* (letterer/photographer); Dan Husted: *Family Circus, RegenSea, Solution* (photographer, letterers unknown)
Page 105: Satoru Nihei: *Beautifool* (designer)
Page 106: Ray Skaines (letterer/photographer)
Page 107: Dan Husted (photographer, letterers unknown)
Page 109: Dan Husted (photographer, letterers unknown)
Page 110: Wanda Driscoll: *Friends* (photographer, letterer unknown); Dan Husted (photographer, letterers unknown)
Page 113: Cindy Fletcher-Holden: *Benbow* (letterer/photographer); Dan Husted: *Dragon* (photographer, letterer unknown); Ray Skaines: *FreeLife* (letterer/photographer)
Page 114: Dan Husted (photographer, letterer unknown)
Page 117: Dan Husted (photographer, letterers unknown)
Page 118: Carla Christopher: *Lady T-Rex* (letterer/ photographer); Dan Husted: *Zoom* (photographer, letterer unknown);
Page 119: Matt Soar: *Thisismyboat* (designer)
Page 120: Joan Ricker (photographer)
Page 121: Drawings by Bud Gillespie
Pages 122–23: Renee Anderson: *Halcyon Days* (letterer/photographer); Carla Christopher: *Grande Finale, Endless Summer* (letterer/photographer); Dan Husted: *Liv Inn, Noah Genda, Old Timer, Silver Lining, Time Out* (photographer, letterers unknown); Lisa Hutchinson: *Got Time? Searenity Now,* (letterer/photographer); Ray Skaines: *Leisure Time, Linger Longer, No Mo Sno, Our Time Out* (letterer/photographer)
Pages 124–25: Renee Anderson: *Foxy Lady, Xtasea* (letterer/photographer); Laurie Churchman: *Cynful Two* (photographer, letterer unknown); Carla Christopher: *Wet Spot* (letterer/photographer); Dan Husted: *C of Love, Hart Strings, Huntress, Insatiable, Love Boat, Perfectly Sue-Ted, Rug Burn, Seaduced, Toucan Go* (photographer, letterers unknown); Lisa Hutchinson: *Double Trouble* (letterer/photographer); Ray Skaines: *Sol Mates, Oooh La La!* (letterer/photographer)